NOBLESVILLE SOUTHE...

W9-BSL-851

0508 01589 894 4

DIMEN QUILTS

PLEASE:

➤ Do NOT mark in book.
➤ Do NOT remove pages.

746.46 Dob 2003
Dobbs, Phyllis M.
Dimensional quilts

PHYLLIS M. DOBBS

Hamilton East Public Library
One Library Plaza
Noblesville, IN 46060

©2003 by Phyllis M. Dobbs
All rights reserved.

No portion of this publication may be reproduced or transmitted in any
form or by any means, electronic or mechanical, including photocopy,
recording, or any information storage and retrieval system, without per-
mission in writing from the publisher, except by a reviewer who may
quote brief passages in a critical article or review to be printed in a maga-
zine or newspaper, or electronically transmitted on radio or television.

Published by
Please call or write for our free catalog of publications. To place an order

krause publications
An F&W Publications Company

700 East State Street • Iola, WI 54990-0001
715-445-2214 • 888-457-2873
www.krause.com

or obtain a free catalog, please call 800-258-0929. Please use our regular
business telephone 715-445-2214 for editorial comment or further information.

Library of Congress Catalog Number 2002113144
ISBN 0-87349-536-5

dedication

To my mother, Jonnie Mae Mitchell, who taught me to sew, gave me fabrics to play with, and later gave me many wonderful heirloom quilts.

and

In loving memory of my grandmother, Penelope White, who quilted an untold number of quilts, some that I now have.

a word of thanks

I owe a big thanks to my husband Danny for his patience, especially since I carried my sewing machine on vacation at the beach and actually used it.

I want to offer my thanks and appreciation to the companies who generously furnished their great products for me to work with:
Expo International, Free Spirit, Hirschberg Schutz Co., Marcus Brothers, Northcott Silk, Inc., Provo Craft, The DMC Corporation, and The Warm Company.

Table of

Contents

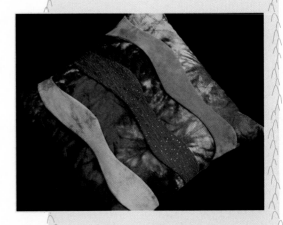

Foreword

Although I am relatively new to the world of quilting, I am somewhat more familiar with the world of quilting books. As a sewing and crafts editor for Krause Publications, I've seen my fair share of quilting manuscripts, photographs, patterns, and diagrams. While each and every quilting book I've been fortunate enough to edit has been a delightful, educational journey, I'm privileged to present Phyllis Dobbs' newest book: *Dimensional Quilts*, as a technical *tour de force*. Here are fresh, simple patterns, vibrant colors, and a new technique that gives these quilts some of the liveliest profiles around. I've learned a great deal from this book … and had fun along the way! I know you will, too.

Christine Townsend

Introduction

The projects in this book are works of *heart* ... as my heart went into each one. They are a combination of a fun-to-stitch techniques and vivid colors.

I have always loved color – wonderful, bright, and exciting color. Colors catch my eye and grab my attention. Fortunately, all these wonderful colors are widely available in fabrics. It was such a delight working on the projects in this book, playing with the fabrics, and coming up with the combinations for each project. I designed most of them backwards, coming up with the fabric combinations first, and then allowing them to inspire me to create the design.

When you are in a store making your fabric selections, pull out bolts of fabric and put them together to come up with combinations pleasing to you. Lay the fabrics across each other. Select prints that blend without being too busy together. If you have a particular fabric in your stash you want to use, but need other fabrics to coordinate, take a swatch to the store with you to help in your selection.

The dimensional technique used in this book gives an added depth to the usual flat quilt and gives the finished project a contemporary look. Some of the patterns are traditional, just stitched in the dimensional method. If you have a favorite pattern, you can use the principles in this book to turn it into a dimensional pattern. This method is fun to sew, and it is deceptively easy and quick to complete your projects.

I designed the patterns in a range from traditional to those that are just for fun with a touch of whimsy. I created the projects to give you an assortment of home decor projects to use throughout your home. The chapters are arranged to focus on different areas of your home, along with some for the baby and some for Christmas.

You will need just some basic sewing supplies, listed in the "Getting Started" chapter. Most of the stitches are straight stitches, which I sewed using my trusty 30-year old White sewing machine. I used a lot of buttons and some beaded fringe for embellishment. I love both buttons and beads and use them whenever I can. It doesn't take many; a few here and there really make a difference in how your completed project looks.

Be sure to read the "Getting Started" chapter before beginning a project. It contains many tips and instructions for the successful completion of your project. It also explains what may appear to be idiosyncrasies in some of the individual instructions. I hope you enjoy selecting the fabrics and are inspired to create many projects using the dimensional technique.

chapter 1

getting started

getting started

Creating dimensional quilts does not require special tools and supplies other than a sewing machine, basic quilting tools, and sewing supplies that you may already have on hand. This chapter reviews the standard tools and supplies that you may need.

If you do not have all of these on hand, purchase them as needed prior to beginning each project. Other supplies that will be needed are listed in the "Materials Needed" list for each project.

Photocopy the patterns from the book. Make several copies of the patterns for which you will need to cut multiple pieces so you can cut more than one at a time.

Basic Supplies

Sewing Machine

A sewing machine will speed up your sewing and will give your finished project a neater appearance. A straight stitch and a zigzag stitch are the only stitches required for the projects in this book.

Sharp Scissors

Good quality scissors with sharp edges will make the cutting easier and give smoother, unfrayed edges. They will also make the cutting less tiring.

Rotary Cutter and Self-healing Cutting Mat

A rotary cutter will save time when cutting out pieces, and will allow you to cut multiple pieces at the same time.

Transparent Quilting Ruler

A quilting ruler is needed for measuring and cutting with the rotary cutter, and for aligning dimensional pieces.

Dressmaking Pins and Pincushion

Pins are needed to secure pieces prior to stitching. A pincushion keeps them together and close at hand.

Iron and Ironing Board

An iron is necessary to press the seams as you sew. Pressing the seams provides uniform seam allowances and gives you the ability to press all the seam allowances in the right direction.

Sewing Needles

Needles will be used to sew the openings closed, to attach the pieces on some of the quilts and to sew on buttons and beaded fringe. You will also need an embroidery needle for the embroidery on some of the items.

Batting

Batting is needed for the quilt and for making the dimensional pieces. I like to work with a cotton or low loft batting, but high loft batting works better on some of the projects.

All Purpose Sewing Threads

Good quality sewing threads in matching colors are needed for machine and hand sewing.

Monofilament (Invisible) Thread

I use this for all quilting. It blends with all colors, taking on the appearance of that color.

Disappearing Ink Pen (Purple)

Use for marking on the fabric where to stop or start stitches, or the points to make a turn. This ink is air soluble and disappears in anywhere from a few hours to a couple of days, depending on humidity.

Seam Ripper

I hope you will not need this but even the best sewers make mistakes. Ripping the seam out with a seam ripper is a lot easier and quicker.

Dimensional Sewing Technique

The basis of dimensional quilting is to take the quilt block or pattern and make it dimensional by using batting to increase the thickness of some of the individual pieces, and placing them on top of the batted background. These pieces are sewn on one edge into the seams of the block, or are tacked or sewn on top of the block. The dimensional pieces are not appliquéd around the edges, but are left loose to give the dimension to the quilt.

Use ¼" seam allowances for all stitching unless otherwise indicated. Press the seams as you sew.

The dimensional pieces will be secured to the surface of the blocks by one of two methods. Each project explains which method was used on that project, but you can choose the other method if you wish.

A tacking stitch is a very simple, hidden stitch that can be used to secure the pieces. Go through the back of the block under the dimensional piece with a needle and thread that has been knotted on one end. Make small, random stitches ½" from the edges of the dimensional piece, catching the bottom fabric of the dimensional piece. Do not stitch through the batting and top fabric.

The other method is to machine stitch the dimensional motif to the block with a topstitch around the edge of the motif.

For the pieces that will be dimensional, cut two pieces of fabric right sides together (rst). Cut one piece of batting the same then layer the two fabric pieces (rst) on top of the batting. Pin the edges together and sew together.

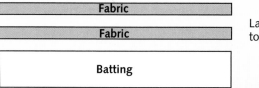

Layer 2 fabrics right sides together on top of batting.

For the pieces that will be stitched into a seam allowance on the base block, do not stitch the edge that will be sewn into the seam allowance. Leave that edge open and turn the piece through this opening, turning through the two pieces of fabric. The batting will then be between the two layers of fabric. Press.

For the pieces that will be sewn entirely onto the block, stitch the seam around the entire piece. Use the scissors to cut a small opening about 1" to 4", depending on the size of the piece to be turned. Cut through the batting and the layer of fabric next to the batting. Make sure you do not cut through the second piece of fabric. Cutting through these two layers, the batting and the next layer of fabric, instead of just through the top layer of fabric, affects the way the seam looks after turning. This method makes the seam fold under and hides it. Turn the piece right side out through this opening. Whipstitch the opening closed, then press.

Completing the Blocks

For the blocks that will have the dimensional pieces stitched in the seam allowance, layer the unstitched edge of the dimensional piece between the two pieces being sewn together, aligning the edges. The two pieces sandwiching the dimensional piece should be (rst). Stitch, then press all seams toward the darker color.

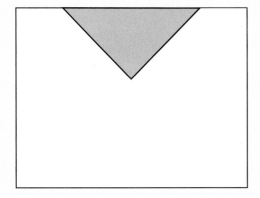

Align dimensional piece to fabric edge right sides together.

Some instructions will direct you to turn a square "on point." In this case, turn the square so that it is at a 45 degree angle with the base square. It will be turned like a diamond on the base square.

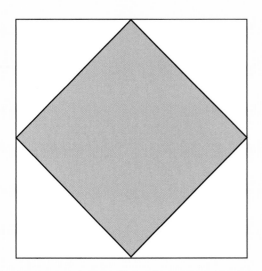

Turn the top block to 45 degree angle for "on point" placement.

General Quilting Instructions

Two methods of constructing the quilt are used in this book. The first method requires binding around the edges. Cut out backing fabric for the quilt and batting 1" larger than the quilt top all the way around. Layer the backing, right side down, the batting and the quilt top, right side up. Leave at least 1" of excess backing and batting all the way around. Pin all three layers together with quilter's safety pins or baste together.

The second method does not use a binding. Cut out backing fabric and batting ½" larger than the quilt top all the way around. Layer the batting and the backing right side up, and the quilt top right side down—the same as the "sandwich" for the dimensional pieces. Pin together and stitch around the edge, leaving a 4" opening along one edge. Trim corners and seams, turn, and press seams. Whipstitch the opening closed.

Individual quilting instructions will be given with each project. Some of the quilt backgrounds will be stipple quilted. Stipple quilting uses continuous random stitching to cover the background. Stitch straight stitches with a free motion of turns and curves to completely cover the background. You can use a darning foot. You can also stipple quilt by lowering the feed dogs or releasing the pressure bar. This will allow you to move the fabric freely as you move and turn it around for stitching.

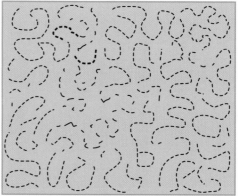

Stipple stitch by quilting curves and turns in a continuous free motion to cover background.

General Binding Instructions

Cut binding strips 1½" wide from the fabric. Sew ends together so that binding is long enough to go around entire quilt edge with 8" left over.

Pin the binding to the quilt back, right sides together. Fold the end of the binding back so that when you start stitching, you stitch first through the folded part. Start along the center of an edge of the quilt, not at a corner. Continue stitching and stop stitching ¼" from the corner edge. Miter the corner by folding the binding strip away from the quilt edge at a perpendicular angle. Fold the binding back down, folding at the edge of the quilt. Resume stitching the next side. Continue stitching to finish all sides and corners the same way.

When you reach the starting point, continue to sew the end across the folded end. Remove from machine and cut off excess binding. Fold binding over the edge toward the top side. Fold under ¼" seam allowance on the unstitched binding edge, press, then pin to the topside of the quilt. Stitch binding to quilt. Remove basting stitches or pins, if applicable.

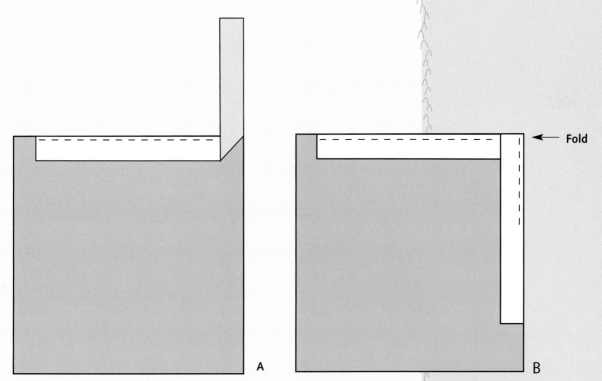

Miter binding corner. A. Stitch to ¼" from end and fold binding straight up. B. Fold straight down with a fold at the edge.

chapter 2

decorating the walls

decorating the walls

PROJECTS

Twisted Log Cabin

Morning Stars

Hearts to You

Squares in Suspense

Flying in Circles

Let's Bloom

Twisted Log Cabin

size: 29" x 29"

materials

¼ yd fuchsia pink fabric

¼ yd violet print fabric

¼ yd green marble fabric

⅓ yd small print fabric

¼ yd large print fabric

2 yds turquoise print fabric

1½ yds high loft batting

4 coordinating green buttons

Coordinating sewing threads

Monofilament invisible thread

✂ cutting

Cut 8 of piece A (3" square), 4 of piece G (9½" square), and 3"- wide border strips from turquoise fabric. This fabric will also be used for the back.

Cut 4 of piece B (4" square) from fuchsia pink fabric.

Cut 4 of piece C (2" x 4") and 4 of piece H (2" x 9½") from purple fabric.

Cut 4 of piece D (2" x 5½") and 4 of piece I (2" x 11") from green marble fabric.

Cut 4 of piece E (2" x 5½") and 4 of piece J (2" x 11"), and 1½" wide strips for binding from small print fabric.

Cut 4 of piece F (2" x 7") and 4 of piece K (2" x 12½") from large print fabric.

construction

1 The instructions are given to complete one block. Repeat with the remaining pieces to form four blocks. Press seams at each step before sewing on another piece.

2 Pin two of piece A right sides together (rst) to the batting and cut batting out. Stitch together. Trim corners and seams. Cut a 1" slit in the batting and the next layer of fabric, turn right side out, and press seams.

3 Sew piece C to one edge of piece B. Sew piece D to the B/C edge. Sew piece E to the B/D edge and piece F to the E/B/C edge. Lay unit right side down on turquoise fabric and cut out back. With (rst), pin these pieces to batting and cut out batting. Stitch together. Trim corners and seams and cut a slit and finish, following step 2.

4 Place the A unit centered and turned on point on top of the log cabin unit. Stitch together at the center by stitching on a button, going through all layers. Take some tacking stitches through the back of the block to catch the bottom layer of the A unit. This has formed the dimensional unit.

5 Sew piece H to one edge of piece G. Sew piece I to the G/H edge. Sew piece J to the I/G edge and piece K to the H/G/J edge. Stitch these four units together making sure that the logs all run in the same direction. Pin a dimensional unit, centered on point, on each of these units. Secure by running tacking stitches through the backside.

6 Sew border strips to the top and bottom edges, then to the side edges. Cut the quilt back and the batting 1" larger than the quilt top all the way around. (See "Getting Started" on page 14.) Quilt ¼" from the edges, stitching around the dimensional block and inside the seam on piece G, and next to the seam on the outer edges of the logs.

7 Sew on binding. (See "Getting Started" on page 15.) Press.

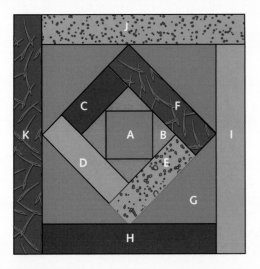

Morning Stars

size: 28½" x 28½"

materials

1½ yds orange tone print fabric
½ yd stripe fabric
⅛ yd blue tonal print fabric
⅓ yd green print fabric

4 red buttons
1 yd cotton batting
Coordinating sewing threads
Monofilament invisible thread

✂ cutting

Cut 8 of piece E, cut 8 of piece B, cut 8 of piece C, and 1½" wide strips for binding from orange tone print fabric. This fabric will also be used for the back.

Cut 4 of piece A and 2½" wide strips for the sashing from green print fabric.

Cut 9 corner blocks 2½" square from blue fabric.

Cut 32 of piece D, reverse pattern and cut 32 more of piece D, and 3" wide strips for the borders from the striped fabric.

∿ construction

1 See patterns on pages 90 and 91. The instructions are given to complete one block. Repeat with the remaining pieces to form four blocks. Press seams at each step before sewing on another piece.

2 Pin two of piece E right sides together (rst) on top of batting and cut batting out. Stitch together. Trim corners and seams. Cut a 1" slit in the batting and the next layer of fabric, turn right side out, and press seams. Repeat with two of piece D, but leave one straight edge unstitched for turning. Stitch eight of the piece D units. Repeat for each block.

3 Pin two of the D units to one edge of piece A, aligning the open edge of piece D to the edge of piece A. The diagonal edges of each D unit should meet at the center of the block. Pin piece B on top of the D units so that B and A pieces are (rst), with the D units sandwiched between them. Stitch together. Repeat with the opposite side of piece A. Repeat on the two remaining edges of piece A, stitching a piece C to these sides.

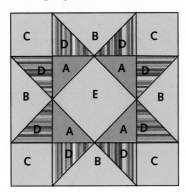

4 Pin the E unit centered on point on top of the block. Sew button in center, going through all layers.

5 Cut 12 sashing strips to 9½" lengths. Join two blocks together with sashing strips to the top and bottom sides of the blocks, then sew strips on the top and bottom ends of the block unit. Repeat with remaining two blocks. Join two sashings together at the ends with corner blocks and add corner blocks on each end. Repeat to form three units. Join the block units together with one of these sashing strips. Sew a sashing strip on each side of this completed unit.

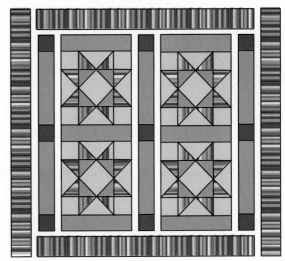

Join blocks, sashings and corner blocks—stitch pieces in a column then sew the columns together on side edges.

6 Sew border strips to the top and bottom edges, then to the side edges. Cut the quilt back and the batting 1" larger than the quilt top all the way around (see "Getting Started" on page 14). Quilt around the stars, around the blocks on the sashing and on the border next to the inside seam.

7 Sew on binding (see "Getting Started" on page 15). Press.

Hearts to You

size: 20½" x 20½"

materials

¼ yd green and white plaid fabric
⅛ yd pink fabric
1 yd green fabric
¼ yd dark pink marbled fabric
⅔ yd low loft batting

7 assorted pink and green buttons
Coordinating sewing threads
Monofilament invisible thread

✂ cutting

Cut 4 rectangles 6½" x 7" from the green plaid fabric.

Cut 6 sashing strips 3" x 7" and 6 sashing strips 3" x 6½" from the green fabric. Use this fabric also for the back.

Cut 8 hearts and 1½" wide binding strips from the dark pink marbled fabric.

Cut 9 square blocks 3" x 3" from the pink fabric.

⚮ construction

1 See pattern on page 92. Join two blocks together with sashing strips to the top and bottom sides of the blocks, then sew strips on the top and bottom ends of the block unit. Repeat with remaining two blocks. Join two sashings together at the ends with corner blocks and add corner blocks on each end. Repeat to form three units. Join the block units together with one of these sashing strips. Sew a sashing strip on each side of this completed unit. See illustration on page 21 for "Morning Star" quilt.

2 Layer two hearts (rst), and pin to top of batting. Cut batting out and sew together. Repeat with remaining hearts. Cut a 1" slit in the batting and the next layer of fabric and turn right side out; press seams. Whipstitch the opening closed.

3 Center a heart on each block and pin to the block. Stitch buttons on hearts going through all layers of fabric and batting. See the photograph for placement. Take some tacking stitches through the back of the block to catch the bottom layer of the hearts about ½" from the edge of the heart.

4 Cut the quilt back and the batting 1" larger than the quilt top all the way around (see "Getting Started" on page 14). Quilt ¼" around the hearts and seams.

5 Sew on binding (see "Getting Started" on page 15). Press.

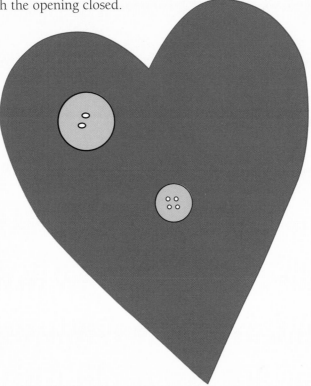

Squares in Suspense

size: 25½" x 25½"

materials

1⅓ yd bright green and print fabric
½ yd blue tonal fabric
½ yd pale blue fabric
¼ yd green and blue print fabric

4 large light green buttons
Coordinating sewing threads
Monofilament invisible thread
1 yd low loft batting

✂ cutting

Cut 8 of piece F, 9 corner blocks 2½" x 2½" and 1½" strips for binding from the bright green print fabric.

Cut 32 piece B, 4 piece E, and 12 sashing strips 2½" x 8½" from the blue tonal print fabric.

Cut 8 of piece C, 8 of piece D, and 2" wide border strips from the pale blue fabric.

Cut 15 of piece A from the green and blue print fabric.

⟅ construction

1 See patterns on pages 94 and 95. The instructions are given to complete one block. Repeat with the remaining pieces to form four blocks. Press seams at each step before sewing on another piece.

2 Sew a piece C to one edge of piece E. Repeat on the opposite side of piece E. Sew a piece D to the other 2 sides of piece E.

3 Layer two of piece B right sides together and pin to batting. Cut batting out and sew together leaving the diagonal edge open. Repeat to form four for each block. Trim seams and corners. Turn right side out and press.

4 Pin a B unit centered on one of the C or D edges, aligning the open edge of the B unit to the edge. Pin piece A on top of the B units and block so that the A pieces and block are (rst), with the B units sandwiched between them. Stitch together. Repeat with each side.

5 Sew sashing to join blocks. See illustration on page 21 in "Morning Stars" quilt.

6 Layer two of piece F right sides together and pin to batting. Cut batting out and sew together. Repeat with remaining F pieces. Trim seams and corners. Cut a 1" slit in the batting and the next layer of fabric; turn right side out and press seams. Whipstitch the opening closed.

7 Center an F unit on point in the center of the block and pin to the block. Stitch a button centered on the F unit going through all layers of fabric and batting.

8 Cut the quilt back and the batting 1" larger than the quilt top all the way around (see "Getting Started" on page 14). Quilt ¼" around the dimensional points (F units) and around the seams.

9 Sew on binding (see "Getting Started" on page 15). Press.

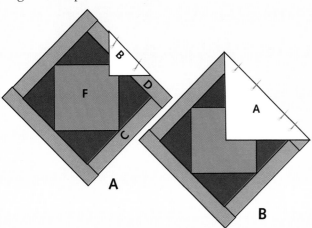

A. Pin dimensional piece to edge of block, right sides together.
B. Pin A piece on top of the dimensional piece, right sides together. Stitch then repeat on remaining edges, starting with the opposite edge.

Flying in Circles

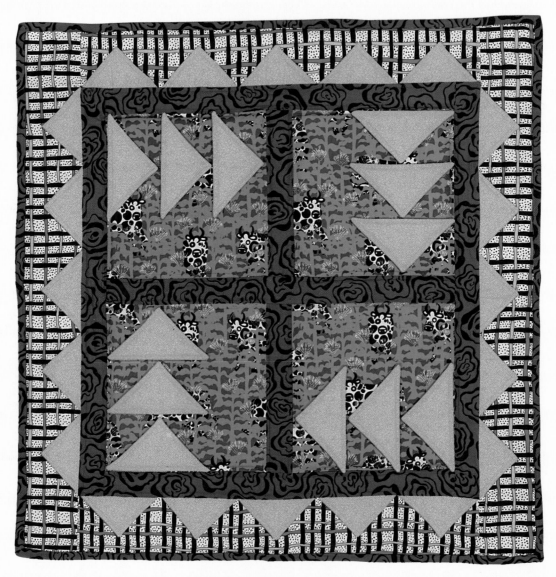

size: 29½" x 29½"

materials

⅔ yd orange tonal print fabric
⅓ yd green print fabric
½ yd purple print fabric
1½ yd plaid fabric

1 yd cotton batting
Coordinating sewing threads
Monofilament invisible thread

✂ cutting

Cut 24 of piece A and 40 of piece B from orange tonal print fabric.

Cut 4 squares 9½" x 9½" from green print fabric.

Cut 1¾" wide strips for inner border and sashing, and 1½" wide strips for binding from purple print fabric.

Cut 3¾" outer border strips from plaid fabric.

construction

1 See pattern on page 93. Layer two of piece A (rst) and pin to top of batting. Cut batting out and sew together all the way around. Repeat with remaining A pieces for a total of 12. Cut a 1" slit in the batting and the next layer of fabric. Trim seams and corners, and turn right side out and press seams. Whipstitch the opening closed.

2 Layer two of piece B (rst) and pin to top of batting. Cut batting out and sew together, leaving the bottom (long) edge of the triangle un-stitched. Repeat with the remaining B pieces for a total of 20. Trim seams and corners; turn and press.

3 Join blocks with purple sashing strips to form a square. Sew purple border strips to the top and bottom edges, and then to the side edges.

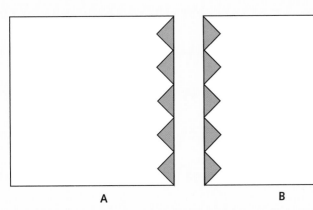

A

B

A. Pin dimensional blocks evenly spaced along one edge. Pin border right sides together over dimensional blocks, stitch and press border and dimensional blocks to the border. B. Repeat on opposite side then remaining sides.

4 Pin five B units along one edge of the quilt block unit, aligning the open edge of B unit to the edge. Pin a plaid border strip on top of the B units and block so that the border and block are (rst), with the B units sandwiched between them. Stitch to-gether. Repeat with the opposite side of the quilt unit, then the remaining two side edges.

5 Pin three A units on each green block. See the photograph for placement. Topstitch the A units to the blocks, stitching ¼" from the edge. Topstitch the B units to the borders, also stitching ¼" from the edge.

6 Cut the quilt back and the batting 1" larger than the quilt top all the way around (see "Getting Started" on page 14). Quilt ¼" around the seams.

7 Sew on binding (see "Getting Started" on page 15). Press.

Let's Bloom

size: 10" x 26"

materials

½ yd green and black print fabric
¼ yd multi-colored stripe fabric
¼ yd yellow marbled fabric
¼ yd green print fabric
⅛ yd dark green fabric
⅛ yd turquoise marbled fabric
⅛ yd orange tonal print fabric

⅛ yd dark rose marbled fabric
½ yd cotton batting
Coordinating sewing threads
Monofilament invisible thread
Steam-a-Seam 2® double stick fusible web
Air soluble disappearing ink pen (purple)

✂ cutting

Note – the pattern pieces are all named with A, B, and C, indicating to which block the pieces go. All the pattern pieces with A form the flower and leaf unit for that block and so on with the B and C pieces.

Cut inner borders and sashing 1½" wide from stripe fabric.
Cut borders 2" wide from green and black print. Use this fabric also for the back.

Cut 3 blocks 6" x 7" from the yellow fabric.
Cut 2 of A from turquoise fabric (one reversed).
Cut 2 of B from orange fabric (one reversed).
Cut 2 of C from dark. rose fabric (one reversed).

Fold green print fabric (rst) and cut two each of A2 right and left pieces, B2 right and left pieces, and C2 right and left pieces. Each pattern will be cut with one piece reversed from the other piece.

construction

1 See patterns on pages 96 and 97. Join the yellow blocks together on the short edges with sashing strips. Then sew sashing strips along the side edges. Sew borders to the top and bottom edges then to the side edges.

2 Layer pattern pieces A, B, C, A2, B2, and C2 (rst) and pin to top of batting. Cut batting out and sew together all the way around. Cut a 1" slit in the top layer of fabric and turn right side out; press seams. Whipstitch the opening closed. Turn and press. To easily identify the pieces when attaching them to the blocks, pin the paper pattern back on the piece until you are ready to sew.

3 Following the instructions of the manufacturer for the fusible web, Cut and fuse pieces A1, B1, and C1 with the dark green fabric to the yellow blocks, aligning the bottom edges. See the photographs for placement. Be sure to reverse the pattern piece when tracing onto the fusible web. Machine appliqué around the edges with the satin zigzag stitch.

4 Pin the flowers pieces, A, B, and C, at the top of the stem pieces, matching letter grouping. Place and pin flowers ¼" over the top edge of the stem. Stitch to the background with two straight lines, radiating from the bottom center in a "V." The width of the top of the "V" will vary depending on the width of the flower. You can draw the stitching lines with the disappearing ink pen.

5 Pin the A2, B2, and C2 pieces in place, aligning to the bottom of the block. Stitch to the background with a single straight line, centered and going from the bottom to the top of the piece.

6 Lay the backing fabric right side up on the batting. Lay the quilt top right side down on top so that the backing and top are (rst). Pin and cut out the backing and batting. Stitch together, leaving a 4" opening along the bottom edge. Trim corners and seams, turn right side out; press. Whipstitch the opening closed.

7 Quilt ¼" around the flowers and leaves, from the seams on the sashing, and around the edge of the quilt.

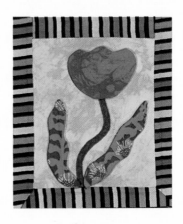

throughout the kitchen

chapter 3

throughout the kitchen

PROJECTS

Something to Crow About
Wall Hanging

Woven Place Mat

Apples of My Eye Chairback

Pinwheels in Motion
Table Runner

Vegetable Patch Centerpiece

Tulip Potholder

Something to Crow About Wall Hanging

size: 17" x 18"

materials

- ⅔ yd yellow tonal print fabric
- ¼ yd orange print fabric
- ⅛ yd turquoise marbled fabric
- ⅛ yd lime green print fabric
- ¼ yd orange plaid fabric
- ¼ yd red and turquoise plaid fabric
- ⅛ yd dark rose marbled fabric

- ⅛ yd yellow plaid fabric
- Turquoise button
- ⅔ yd cotton batting
- Coordinating sewing threads
- Monofilament invisible thread
- Steam-a-Seam 2® double stick fusible web

cutting

Cut rectangle block 13½" x 12" from the yellow fabric. This fabric will also be used for the back.

Cut 2 of piece A (with one of them reversed) from orange print fabric.

Cut 2 of piece B (with one reversed) from turquoise fabric.

Cut 2 of piece C (with one reversed) from red and turquoise plaid fabric.

Cut 2 of piece D (with one reversed) from lime green print fabric.

Cut 2 of piece E (with one reversed) from orange plaid fabric.

Cut 2 of piece F, K and H (with one of each reversed) from dark rose fabric.

Cut 2 of piece G (with one reversed) from yellow plaid fabric. This fabric will also be used for the appliqué for the legs, with instructions given later.

Cut border strips 2" wide from the various fabrics above. You may want to cut your borders last so that you can arrange your border fabrics around the block to get the most pleasing combination prior to cutting.

construction

1 See patterns on pages 98 and 99. Layer pieces A, B, C, D, E, F, G, and H (rst), and pin to top of batting. Cut batting out and sew together all the way around on pieces A and K. Leave the flat ends of B, C, D, and E open. Leave the straighter edge of F open, the short edge of G open, and the inside curve of H open. For the A and K pieces, cut a 1" slit in the top layer of fabric, trim seams and points and clip inner curves. Turn right side out and press seams. Whipstitch the opening closed. For the remaining pieces, trim seams and clip inside curves. Turn through the opening and press.

2 Lay the body (A) and the feathers, starting with B at the top and going down to E, for placement on the yellow block. Following the manufacturer's instructions for the fusible web, fuse the legs (pieces I and J) to the block so that they will be ¼" under the body. Be sure to reverse the patterns when tracing on the fusible web. Machine appliqué around the edges with the satin zigzag stitch, using matching thread.

3 Pin the body to the block. Pin the tail feathers so that the ends are ¼" under the body. Pin the beak (piece G) under the head front and pin piece F under the beak underneath the neck edge. Pin piece H on top of the head with the edge under the body. All pieces should be tucked ¼" under the body. See photograph for placement. Topstitch the body to the block ⅛" from the edge,

being sure to stitch over the ends of the attached pieces as you stitch. Stitch a straight line centered on top of the tail feathers half of the length beginning at the end next to the body.

4 Pin dimensional unit K (wings) on top of the body. Stitch to the body with two straight lines (see the pattern for stitching line placement).

5 Two rows of borders will be stitched on in a log cabin method. Lay fabrics around outside of block to get most pleasing arrangement of fabrics and cut strips 2" wide. Sew the first border strip to the top edge of the block, with the next piece stitched to the right side, then the bottom edge and then the left edge. Repeat with the second row of borders around the edge.

6 Sew button for eye.

7 Lay the backing fabric right side up on the batting. Lay the quilt top right side down on the backing so that the backing and top are (rst). Pin and cut out the backing and batting. Stitch together, leaving a 4" opening along the bottom edge. Trim corners and seams. Turn right side out, press, and whipstitch the opening closed.

8 Quilt ¼" around the rooster, the seams and around the edge of the quilt.

Woven Place Mat

size: 12" x 17"

materials

½ yd black fabric

¼ yd bright pink print fabric

¼ yd bright yellow print fabric

¼ yd lime green print fabric

¼ yd bright blue print fabric

½ yd low loft batting

Coordinating sewing threads

✂ cutting

Cut rectangle block 9½" x 14½" and 2½" wide
    border strips from black fabric. This fabric
    will also be used for the back.
Cut 4 strips 2½" x 14½" from the pink fabric.

Cut 2 strips 2½" x 14½" from the blue fabric.
Cut 6 strips 2½" x 9½" from the lime green fabric.
Cut 4 strips 2½" x 9½" from the yellow fabric.

⚲ construction

1 Layer 2 of the same colored strips (rst), and
pin to batting. Repeat for all strips. Cut batting out and sew together on the long side edges,
leaving the ends open. Trim seams; turn right side
out, and press.

2 Lay the strips on the black block, evenly
spaced. See the photograph for placement.
Pin the ends to the edges across the top and on
one side. Weave the strips over and under and pin
on the remaining edges. Sew ends in place.

3 Pin the border strips to the top and bottom
edges, (rst), and stitch. Repeat with the side
edges.

4 Lay the backing fabric right side up on the
batting. Lay the quilt top right side down on
top so that the backing and top are (rst). Pin and
cut out the backing and batting. Stitch together,
leaving a 4" opening along the bottom edge. Trim
corners and seams. Turn, press, and whipstitch
the opening closed.

5 Topstitch around the inside edge of the
border.

Note

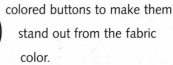

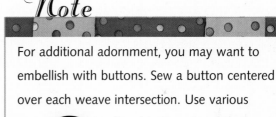

For additional adornment, you may want to
embellish with buttons. Sew a button centered
over each weave intersection. Use various
colored buttons to make them
stand out from the fabric
color.

Apples of My Eye Chairback

size: 13½" x 15½"

 materials

⅓ yd red fabric
½ yd red and blue plaid fabric
¼ yd blue stripe print fabric
Scraps green fabric

½ yd low loft batting
Coordinating sewing threads
Monofilament invisible thread

✂ cutting

Cut 12 of the apple (cut 6 of these reversed), 1½" wide inner border strips, and four strips for the ties 2½" x 23" from the red fabric.

Cut 12 leaves (cut 6 of these reversed) from the green fabric.

Cut a rectangle block 10" x 8½" from the stripe fabric.

Cut 2½" wide outer border strips from the plaid fabric.

construction

1 See pattern on page 100. Lay 2 of the apple pieces right sides together and pin to batting. Repeat for all apple and leaf pieces. Cut batting out and sew apple units together. Trim seams and points and clip inside curves. Cut a 1" slit in the batting and the next layer of fabric and turn right side out and press seams. Whipstitch the opening closed. Sew the leaves together, leaving the flat edge opposite of the point open. Trim seams and points. Turn and press.

2 Sew red inside border strips to the side edges of the stripe block, then sew red border strips to the top and bottom edges. Sew plaid border strips to the side edges then to the top and bottom edges.

3 Place apples on stripe block, evenly spaced. See the photograph for placement. Pin in place and tuck the open end of leaves ¼" under the apples and pin. Come through the back of the fabric and take tacking stitches through the bottom layer of fabric for the apples and leaves to secure them in place.

4 Fold the ties in half lengthwise and sew together on the open side edges and across one end. Trim corners, turn right side out and press.

5 Lay the backing fabric right side up on the batting. Pin two of the unstitched ends of the ties to the top left and right edges. Align so that the ends and the sides match. Lay the quilt top right side down on top so that the backing and top are (rst) with the ties between them. Pin and cut out the backing and batting. Stitch together, leaving a 4" opening along the bottom edge. Trim corners and seams. Turn, press, and whipstitch the opening closed.

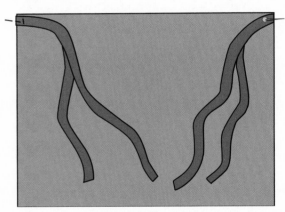

Pin two ties (open ends) to each corner.

6 Topstitch around apples and ¼" on the outside edges of the red border seams.

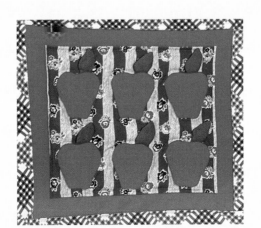

Pinwheels in Motion Table Runner

size: 43" x 15"

materials

1 yd green tonal print fabric
⅓ yd blue fabric
⅓ yd blue and green plaid fabric

½ yd blue and white floral fabric
½ yd low loft batting
12 green buttons

✂ cutting

Cut 24 of piece A from the blue and green plaid
fabric.

Cut 12 of piece B from the blue fabric.

Cut 12 of piece B and 1½" wide binding strips
from the green tonal fabric. Also use this fabric for the back.

Cut 2 sashings 3½" x 12", and border strips 2"
wide from the blue and white floral fabric.

construction

1 See pattern on page 101. Layer two of piece A
(rst), and pin to batting. Cut batting out and
sew together. Repeat with remaining A pieces for a
total of 12 dimensional units. Cut a 1" slit in the
batting and the next layer of fabric. Trim seams
and corners, turn right side out, and press seams.
Whipstitch the opening closed.

2 With (rst), sew one blue piece B and one
green piece B together on the diagonal edge to
form a square. Repeat with the remaining pieces
for a total of 12 units. Sew these together in
groups of four to form a total of three squares,
making sure the colors alternate.

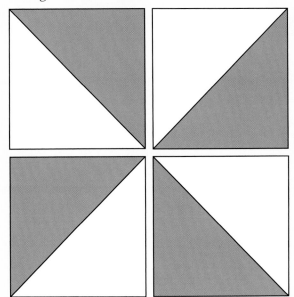

Placement of units to form block.

3 Join blocks in a strip with the sashing strips.
See photograph for placement. Sew border
strips to the ends then on the side edges.

4 Pin the plaid dimensional triangles on top of
the blue areas so that they form a point toward the middle of the block. Again, refer to the
photograph. Attach a button in the center of the
dimensional piece, going through all layers. Also
go through the background fabric and sew tacking
stitches to catch the bottom layer of the dimensional piece.

5 Cut the quilt back and the batting 1" larger
than the quilt top all the way around (see
"Getting Started" on page 14). Quilt ¼" around
the seam in the remaining visible blue area and
from the seams on the sashing strips. Stipple
stitch to cover the green sections of the pinwheel
(see "Getting Started" on page 14).

6 Sew on binding (see "Getting Started" on page
15). Press.

Vegetable Patch Centerpiece

size: 21½" x 21½"

materials

¼ yd red chili print fabric
⅓ yd green cabbage print fabric
½ yd yellow marbled fabric
⅔ yd red and yellow pepper print fabric

1¼ yd green pea print fabric
⅔ yd cotton batting
1 large yellow button

✂ cutting

Cut 2 from the red chili fabric, 5½" squares.
Cut 2 from the green cabbage fabric, 10½" squares.
Cut 2 from the yellow fabric, 12½" squares.

Cut 2 from the red and yellow pepper fabric, 21" squares.
Cut 2 from the green pea fabric, 22½" squares.

construction

1 See patterns on pages 102 and 103. Layer 5½" red squares (rst), and pin to batting. Cut batting out and sew together. Trim seams and corners. Repeat with the 12½" yellow squares, and with the 22½" green pea square. For the red and yellow squares, cut a 1" to 4" slit, depending on the size of the square, in the batting and the next layer of fabric. Cut the slits in the center of the blocks. Trim seams and corners, turn right side out, and press seams. Whipstitch the opening closed. For the green pea square, cut a slit from the top fabric side instead of the batting and next layer. All the blocks will be stacked on each other with the slit facing down, except for the green pea layer. This will be the bottom layer and will have the slit facing up, and covered by the other squares.

2 Pin the 10½" cabbage green print squares (rst). Pin the template using pattern A along an edge and cut out the serpentine line. Repeat on each side of the block. Repeat this step with the 21" red and yellow pepper fabric, using pattern B as the template. (Note that pattern B is shown in half-length and should be flipped over at the fold line to finish tracing the line on one side.) Repeat with the remaining sides. Then place these two blocks on batting as in step 1 above, and follow those instructions to sew block and cut opening. Trim seams and clip inside curves before turning. Press.

3 See the photograph for placement. Center the red chili block on top of the cabbage green block, and pin. Topstitch the red block ¼" from edge, stitching through all layers. Then place this unit on top of the yellow block and pin. Secure these blocks together by topstitching on the green fabric ¼" from the edge of the red block. Leave the scalloped edges loose.

4 Repeat this process by stacking the unit centered on the red and yellow pepper block. Stitch on the yellow block, going through all layers, ¼" from the edge. Finally, stack the unit on the green pea block. Stitch on the pepper fabric, ¼" from the edge of the yellow block. Stitch around outside edge of the green pea block, ¼" from the edge.

5 Sew the yellow button so it is centered on the red chili square.

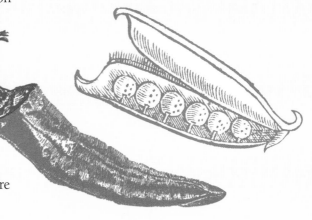

Tulip Potholder

size: 8½" x 8½"

materials

¼ yd green tonal print
¼ yd green print
⅛ yd fuchsia tonal print
Scraps orange marbled print

¼ yd cotton batting
Coordinating sewing threads
Monofilament invisible thread

cutting

Cut 8½" square from the green fabric. This will also be used for the back.

Cut 2 of piece A, 2 of piece B and 1½" wide strips for binding from the green print fabric.

Cut 6 of piece C from the fuchsia fabric.

Cut 6 of piece D from the orange fabric.

construction

1 See pattern on page 104. Layer two of piece A right sides together (rst) and pin to batting. Cut batting out and sew together. Repeat with remaining B and C pieces. Trim seams and points. Cut a 1" slit in the batting and the next layer of fabric; turn right side out and press seams. Whipstitch the opening closed. Repeat with piece D, except when sewing leave the shorter bottom edges open. Trim seams and point; turn and press.

2 Cut the quilt back and the batting the same size as the green square. Sew on binding (see "Getting Started" on page 15). Press.

3 Place the flowers and triangles on the top of the green block. See the photograph for placement. The open end of the orange tips should be centered ¼" under the fuchsia tulips. The large triangle should be turned point down. The small triangle should be turned point up and placed under the point of the large triangle. Pin each piece in place once the arrangement is complete. Topstitch everything in place except for the orange points. Stitch ⅛" from edges.

chapter 4

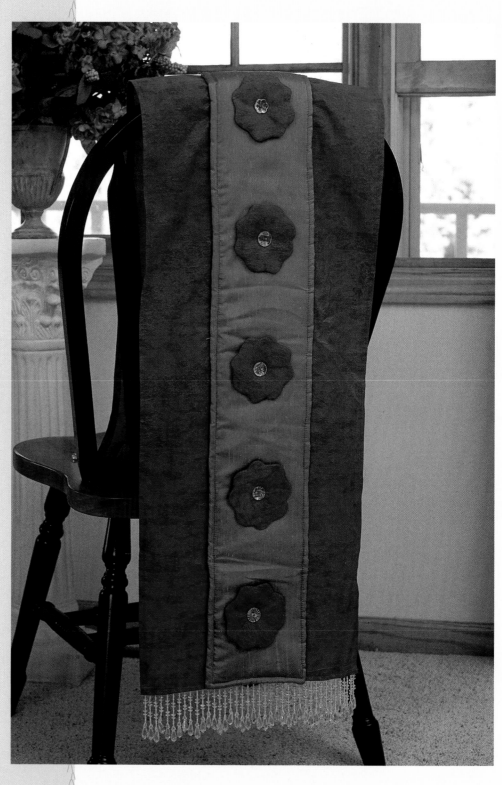

dining room elegance

PROJECTS

Spring Flowers Table Runner

Diamond and Squares
Buffet Scarf

Mardi Gras Place Mat

Puff Flowers Chair Panel

Spring Flowers Table Runner

size: 42" x 11½"

materials

1 yd lime green silk fabric

⅔ yd emerald green silk fabric

25" of lime green beaded fringe (Trimtations # IR19766R)

½ yd low loft batting

DMC 6-stranded cotton embroidery floss, colors 911, 3609, and 3607

Embroidery needle

Coordinating sewing threads

Monofilament invisible thread

Disappearing ink pen

✂ cutting

Cut 2 strips 43" x 5¾" and 1 strip 43" x 2½" from
   the lime green fabric. This fabric will also be
   used for the back.
Cut 28 of piece A from the emerald green fabric.

⚟ construction

1 See pattern on page 105. Layer two of piece A
   (rst), and pin to the batting. Cut the batting
out and sew together, leaving the long edge open.
Repeat with remaining A pieces for a total of 14
dimensional triangles. Trim seams and corners.
Turn and press.

2 Lay seven of the dimensional triangles on one
   strip of the 5¾"-wide lime green strips, aligning edges so the open end of the triangle matches
the edge of the strip. Repeat with the remaining
strip. Sew edges together.

Pin dimensional units spaced along one edge. Align open
ends with edge. Place 2½" strip right sides together on
top and stitch.

3 Lay the 2½" wide strip on top of one of the
   strips with the triangles. Align the edges on
the side with the triangles (rst). Stitch together.
Join the strip on the triangle edge the same way to
the other side of the 2½" wide strip. Press.

4 Trace the embroidery stitches on the center
   strip using a disappearing ink pen. The embroidery floss is divisible into six strands. Use
three strands for the embroidery. (See the instructions for the embroidery in the section
"Embroidery Stitches" on page 88) The stitches
used are the lazy daisy, colonial knot, and the
feather stitch. The feather stitches are stitched
with DMC floss color 911,
the lazy daisies with floss
color 3607, and the colo-
nial knots with 3609.

5 Lay the backing fabric right side up on top of
   the batting. Lay the quilt top right side down
on top so that the backing and top are (rst). Pin,
and cut out the backing and batting. Sandwich
fringe between the front and back layers on each
end of the table runner, and pin. Fringe edge
should be aligned with the edge of the fabric.
Stitch together, leaving a 4" opening along a side
edge. Trim corners and seams. Turn, press, and
whipstitch the opening closed.

6 Quilt on the lime green layer ⅓" around the
   dimensional triangles and around the outside
edge.

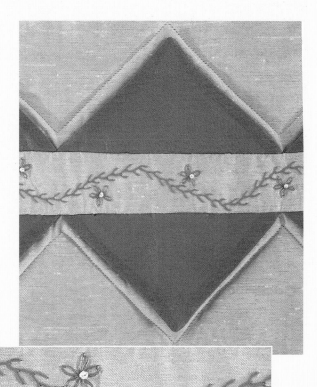

Diamond and Squares Buffet Scarf

size: 50" x 12"

materials

1½ yds light gray silk fabric
½ yd deep green silk fabric
¼ yd purple silk fabric
1½ yds cotton batting

3 large mother of pearl buttons (antique buttons were used in model)
Coordinating sewing threads
Monofilament invisible thread

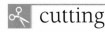 cutting

Cut 2 from the light gray fabric 12½" x 52". One
of these pieces will be used for the back.
Cut 12 of piece A from the dark green fabric.
Cut 6 of piece B from the purple fabric.

construction

1 See pattern on page 107. Layer two of piece A
(rst), and pin to batting. Cut batting out and
sew together. Repeat with remaining A pieces and
with the B pieces. Trim seams and corners. Cut a
1" slit in the batting and the next layer of fabric.
Turn right side out, and press seams. Whipstitch
the opening closed.

2 Fold each end of the light gray strips to form
a point. Fold so that the side edges meet.
Press fold lines and use this as the cutting line for
the points.

**Fold ends down at a 45 degree angle and press to get
cutting lines for points.**

3 Layer the two light gray strips (rst) and pin to
batting. Cut the batting out; sew together,
leaving a 4" opening along one edge. Trim seams
and corners. Turn, whipstitch the opening closed,
and press.

4 Arrange the green dimensional triangles on
the front of the light gray scarf. Measure to
ensure that they are each centered. Leave 1½" between the flat edges of the triangles. See the photograph for placement. Stitch the triangles to the
scarf, stitching ¼" from the edge.

5 Center the purple dimensional squares, on
point, on top of the triangles. Stitch the
squares to the scarf, stitching ¼" from edge.

6 Quilt ¼" around the triangles and squares and
¼" from edge of scarf.

7 Sew buttons to the center of the squares.

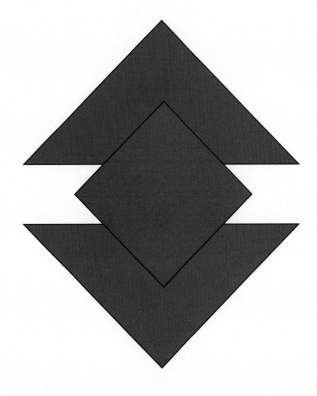

Mardi Gras Place Mat

size: 13" x 18"

materials

½ yd purple silk fabric
½ yd gold silk fabric
½ yd cotton batting

24 crystal rochaille beads
Coordinating sewing threads
Monofilament invisible thread

✂ cutting

Cut 16 of the piece A and 2 rectangles,
  9½" x 12½". from the purple fabric.
Cut 2 rectangles, 13½" x 18½", from the gold
  fabric.

construction

1 See pattern on page 100. Layer two of piece A right sides together (rst), and pin to batting. Cut batting out and sew together, leaving the long edge open. Repeat with remaining A pieces. Trim seams and points; turn and press.

2 Pin four dimensional triangles (A) to a long edge of the purple rectangle. Align edges so that the open ends of the triangles line up with the edge of the rectangle, and the triangles are pointed toward the center of the rectangle. Stitch along the edge to secure triangles. Repeat with the other side. See the illustration on page 47 for the "Spring Flowers Table Runner."

3 Lay the remaining purple rectangle on top of the one with the triangles, (rst). The triangles will be sandwiched between the two rectangle layers. Pin this unit to batting, and cut batting out. Stitch together. Trim seams and corners. Cut a 3" slit in the batting and the next layer of fabric and turn right side out and press seams. Whipstitch the opening closed.

4 Layer the two gold rectangles (rst) and pin to batting. Cut batting out and sew together. Trim seams and corners. Cut a 2" slit in the center of the top layer of fabric (not in the batting and the next layer). This will be the top side, and the slit will be covered.

5 Center the purple unit on top of the gold rectangle and pin in place. Topstitch ⅓" from seam on the purple unit. Quilt ⅓" from outer edge of the place mat.

6 Sew three crystal beads to the purple triangles, one at the point and one on each side at the base of the triangle, next to the seam.

Puff Flowers Chair Panel

size: 57½" x 13½"

materials

- 1¾ yd iridescent wine fabric
- 1¾ yd iridescent grey fabric (with wine cast)
- 1¾ yd low loft batting
- 28" crystal beaded fringe (Trimtations IR1988CAB)

- 9 assorted ¾" glass buttons (antique buttons were used in model)
- Coordinating sewing threads
- Monofilament invisible thread

cutting

Cut one strip 14½" x 58½" and 18 of piece A
　　from the wine fabric.
Cut 2 strips 6½" x 58" from the gray fabric.

construction

1 See pattern on page 100. Layer two of piece A
(rst), and pin to batting. Cut batting out and
sew together. Repeat with remaining A pieces.
Trim seams and clip inside curves. Cut a 1" slit in
the batting and the next layer of fabric; turn right
side out and press seams. Whipstitch the opening
closed.

2 Layer the two gray strips (rst) and construct
following #1 above.

3 Turn a double hem ¼" under on the sides of
the wine strip and stitch. Repeat for the ends.
(To make a double hem, turn under ¼", and then
again ¼".)

4 Lay the gray strip centered lengthwise on top
of the wine strip and pin. Stitch together on
the gray strip ¼" from edge all the way around.

5 Arrange the flowers along the strip approxi-
mately 2¾" apart. See the photograph for
placement. When you have the flowers spaced
evenly, pin them to the panel. Secure the flowers
by stitching buttons in the centers, stitching
through all layers.

6 Whipstitch the beaded fringe to the panel
ends. Stitch the tape holding the fringe to the
back of the hem.

throughout the house

chapter 5

throughout the house

PROJECTS

Ocean Waves Pillow

A Single Blossom Pillow

Blooms Valance

Let's Play Picnic Basket

In My Garden Cafe Curtains

Geometrics Mantle Scarf

Crazy Footstool

Ocean Waves Pillow

size: 13½" x 13½"

materials

½ yd blue and green tie dyed fabric
⅛ yd violet print fabric
⅛ yd lime green marbled fabric
⅛ yd turquoise marbled fabric
½ yd low loft batting

14" pillow form
½ yd muslin
Coordinating sewing threads
Monofilament invisible thread

 cutting

Cut a 14½" x 14½" square from the blue and green tie dyed fabric. This fabric will also be used for the back.

Cut 2 of piece 1 from turquoise fabric (reverse 1 of the pieces).

Cut 2 of piece 2 from violet fabric (reverse 1 of the pieces).

Cut 2 of piece 3 from the lime green fabric (reverse 1 of the pieces).

construction

1 See pattern on page 114. Lay two of piece 1 right sides together (rst) and pin to batting. Cut batting out and sew together on the side edges. Leave the ends unstitched. Repeat with the 2 and 3 pieces. Trim seams.

2 Lay batting on top of muslin; put the square tie-dyed fabric right side up on the batting and pin. Cut out the batting and muslin to the same size as the square. Stipple quilt the surface of this "sandwich." See "Getting Started" on page 14. Trim edges to square pillow top.

3 Pin wave strips on the square stippled block in a one-two-three order (with 1 at the top). See photograph for the placement of the waves. Stitch the waves to the block on the side edges to secure the waves.

4 Lay the quilted top (rst) with the backing fabric. Pin and cut out back. Sew together, leaving a 10" opening along one edge. Trim seams and corners. Turn and press. Stuff with pillow form and whipstitch opening closed.

A Single Blossom Pillow

size: 16" x 16"

materials

½ yd lime green pique fabric
⅓ yd bright pink pique fabric
⅓ yd emerald green pique fabric
½ yd of muslin
½ yd low loft batting

Yellow and gold rochaille beads
16" pillow form
Coordinating sewing threads
Monofilament invisible thread

✂ cutting

Cut a 10½" square from the emerald green fabric

Cut 2 of flowers (A) from bright pink. Note that the pattern should be placed on the fold for each piece.

Cut 3½" wide border strips and 2 of piece B from the lime green fabric. This fabric will also be used for the pillow back.

✎ construction

1 See pattern on page 106. Layer the two piece A flowers (rst), and pin to batting. Cut batting out and sew together. Repeat with the B pieces. Trim seams and corners and clip inside points. Cut a 1" slit in the batting and the next layer of fabric, and turn right side out. Press seams. Whipstitch the opening closed.

2 Sew a lime green border strip to one edge of the emerald square, then repeat on the opposite side. Sew border strips to the remaining two edges.

3 Center the flower onto the green block and pin. Stitch together, ¼" from the edge of the flower. Pin the lime green hexagon centered on the flower. Sew together by sewing on a cluster of yellow and gold rochaille beads at the center, sewing through all layers.

4 Lay batting on top of muslin, then put the quilt top right side up on the batting and pin. Cut out the batting and muslin to the same size as the quilt top. Quilt on the flower ¼" from the hexagon edge, on the emerald green fabric around the flower ¼" from the flower edge, and on the lime green border ¼" from the seam.

5 Lay the quilted "sandwich" (rst) with the backing fabric. Pin, and cut out back. Sew together, leaving a 9" opening on the bottom edge. Trim seams and corners. Turn right side out and press. Stuff with pillow form, and whipstitch the opening closed.

Blooms Valance

size: 40½" x 14"

materials

⅔ yd lime green print fabric
⅓ yd bright pink plaid fabric
⅔ yd blue print fabric
½ yd blue stripe fabric
½ yd blue, rose and lime green plaid fabric
½ yd cotton batting

9 lime green buttons
4 yellow buttons
Coordinating sewing threads
Monofilament invisible thread
Air soluble disappearing ink pen (purple)

cutting

Cut 32 of piece A from the blue striped fabric.

Cut 4 of piece B and 5 strips 4½" x 5" for the top loops from the pink plaid fabric.

Cut 16 of piece C and 4 strips 4½" x 5" for the top loops from the lime green fabric.

Cut 2" wide strips for the sashings and inner borders from the blue, rose, and lime green fabric.

Cut 1¾" wide strips for the outer borders from the blue print fabric. This fabric will also be used for the back.

construction

1 See pattern on page 108. Layer two of piece A (rst), and pin to batting. Cut batting out, and sew together, leaving the bottom straight edge open. Repeat with remaining A pieces. Trim seams and corners; clip inside points and curves. Turn and press.

2 Lay a dimensional unit A on a pattern piece B. Align edges so that the open end of the dimensional piece is centered evenly on the edge of the block and the unit lays on top of piece B. The curved edges of the dimensional unit will be toward the center of piece B. Pin. Lay piece C on top of these pieces, (rst) with piece B. Align the diagonal edge of piece C with the straight edge of piece B over the dimensional piece, and pin.

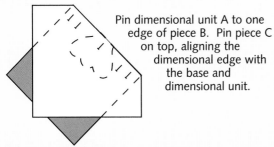

Pin dimensional unit A to one edge of piece B. Pin piece C on top, aligning the dimensional edge with the base and dimensional unit.

Stitch together, stopping and starting ¼" from the ends. Make a dot at the beginning and ending points with a disappearing ink pen to help with your starting and stopping measurements. Repeat on each side of the square. Pin side edges of C

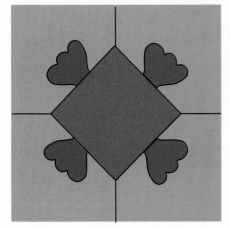

pieces together and start stitching ¼" from the end next to piece B, stitching out. Repeat with the remaining pieces to form four blocks.

Placement of pieces of completed block.

3 Come from back of block and make tacking stitches catching the back fabric of the dimensional units. Sew a button to center of each unit.

4 Join blocks together on the side edges with sashing strips. Sew inner border strips to each end then to the top and bottom edges.

5 Sew outer border strips to the side ends, then to the top and bottom edges.

6 Fold the loops (4½" x 5" pieces, rst) on the long edge. Sew together on the long open edge. Press seam flat so that it goes down the center. Fold ends back on one end to form a point. See instructions and illustration on page 49 for making a point for the Diamond and Square Buffet Scarf. Press and use the fold line as a cutting line. Stitch ¼" from cut edge for the point. Trim points and seams; turn and press.

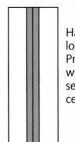

Hanging loops. Press with seam centered.

7 Pin the loops, evenly spaced and alternating colors, across the top edge of the valance. Pin the loops right side up laying on the right side of the valance. Align the open end of the loops to the top edge of the valance, points facing downward.

8 Lay the backing fabric right side up on the batting. Lay the quilt top right side down so that the backing and top are (rst). The loops will be sandwiched between the two layers. Fold the loops at each end toward the center of the valance and pin to prevent catching them in the side seams. Pin and cut out the backing and batting. Stitch together, leaving a 4" opening along the bottom edge. Trim corners and seams. Turn, and press. Whipstitch the opening closed.

9 Quilt ¼" from the edge on the center pink plaid block, from the seams of the lime green blocks, from the outside seam on the outer border strips, and from the outside edge of the valance.

10 Fold loops down overlapping the top of the valance by 1". Sew buttons centered on the points. See photograph for placement.

Let's Play Picnic Basket

size: 12½" x 16½"

(size will vary according to picnic basket used)

materials

½ yd yellow dot fabric

⅛ yd fuchsia marbled fabric

⅛ yd lime green print fabric

⅛ yd rose, blue, and lime green plaid fabric

½ yd cotton batting

½ yd muslin fabric

Picnic basket

6 yellow buttons

✂ cutting

Cut piece 13½" x 17" for the basket top, and 2 pieces 4" x 17" for the end pockets from the yellow dot fabric. If your picnic basket top is a different size, measure the top dimensions and add 1" to the width and length for your cutting size for the top. For the end pockets, cut 5" x the basket width (the shorter edges of the basket top) plus 1".

Cut 12 of piece B from the fuchsia fabric.
Cut 12 of piece A from the lime green fabric.
Cut 4 of piece A from the rose, blue, and lime green plaid fabric.

⚘ construction

1 See pattern on page 109. Layer two of piece A (rst), and pin to batting. Cut batting out and sew together. Repeat with remaining A pieces and with B pieces. Trim seams and corners. Cut a 1" slit in the batting and the next layer of fabric, and turn right side out. Press seams. Whipstitch the opening closed.

2 Lay the batting on top of the muslin, then lay the larger yellow piece right side up on the batting, and pin. Cut out the batting and muslin to the same size as the yellow piece. Stipple quilt the surface of this "sandwich." (See "Getting Started" on page 14.) Trim edges to square.

3 Arrange the pieces on top of the quilted piece. See the illustration below and the photograph for placement. When you have the arrangement evenly spaced, pin in place. Topstitch the pieces to the basket cover, stitching ⅛" around edges.

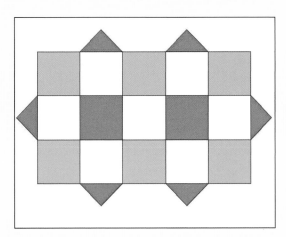

Placement of blocks on basket cover.

4 Sew buttons centered on the six outside squares.

5 Fold a double ¼" hem on one long edge of each basket pocket and stitch. Lay the basket pockets, (rst), on each side edge of the basket top piece, matching the long edge of the pocket without the hem to the side edge. Stitch together along the bottom, top, and side edges. Turn and press. Press under a hem on the basket top to form an even edge on the top and bottom edges between the pockets and stitch.

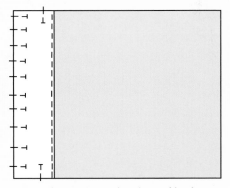

Pin pocket (rst) to side edges of basket top.

6 Slip the pockets over the ends of the basket top.

In My Garden Cafe Curtains

size: 20½" x 17"
(each panel)

materials

1 yd fuchsia stripe fabric
⅔ yd lime green tonal print fabric
¼ yd fuchsia tonal print
¼ yd orange marbled fabric
14 yellow buttons
4 bright pink buttons
Coordinating sewing threads

Monofilament invisible thread
Disappearing ink pen (purple)
* 1 yd cotton batting (optional)
* I did not put batting in the curtain so that it would be lighter weight to push open to the sides. However, if you will be hanging your curtain and not sliding it open, you can use batting for the entire curtain and flowers.

✂ cutting

Cut 2 pieces 10½" x 21½" and 2 pieces, 2½" x 21½", from the pink striped fabric. This fabric will also be used for the backs.

Cut 2 pieces 5½" x 21½", and 10 pieces 4½" x 5" for the loops from the lime green fabric.

Cut 8 pieces of piece A flower from the fuchsia tonal fabric.

Cut 8 pieces of piece A flower from the marbled orange fabric.

construction

1 See pattern on page 109. Pin two flower pieces (rst), and sew together. Repeat with remaining flower pieces for a total of four fuchsia and four orange flowers. Trim seams and clip inside points. Cut a 1" slit in one of the fabric sides, turn right side out, and press seams. Whipstitch the opening closed.

2 Sewing the 21½" edges, join the 10½" high fuchsia striped fabric to the green strip. Sew the 2½" high fuchsia striped piece to the remaining edge of the green strip. Repeat for the second panel.

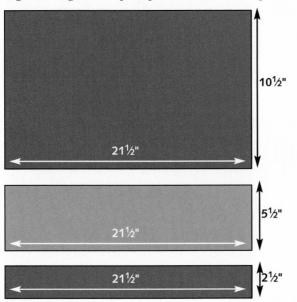

Arrangement for stitching strips to form curtain panel.

3 Arrange the flowers on the green strip, alternating flower colors. See the photograph for placement. Pin in place when you have them evenly spaced. Use circle pattern and disappearing ink pen to trace a circle centered on flowers to use as the stitching guide. Stitch flowers to the panels on the circle line.

4 Fold the lime green loops (4¼" x 5" pieces, rst) on the long edge. Sew together on the long open edges. Press seam flat so that it goes down the center. See illustration on page 61 for the Blooms Valance. Fold ends back on one end to form a point. See instructions and illustration on page 49 for the Diamond and Square Buffet Scarf for making a point. Press and use the fold line as a cutting line. Stitch ¼" from the cut edge for the point. Trim points and seams; turn right side out and press.

5 Pin the loops, evenly spaced, across the top edge of the curtain panels. Pin the loops right side up laying on the right side of the panel, and align the open end of the loops to the top edge of the panels with the points facing downward.

6 Pin the panel (rst) on the backing; pin and cut out backing. The loops will be sandwiched between the two layers. Fold the loops on each end toward the center of the valance and pin to prevent catching them in the side seams. Stitch together, leaving a 4" opening along the bottom edge. Trim corners and seams. Turn, press, and whipstitch the opening closed.

7 Topstitch ¼" from both sides of the seams joining the green and fuchsia fabric and around the outside edges of the panels.

8 Fold loops down, overlapping the top of the valance by 1". Sew yellow buttons centered on the points to hold in place. See photograph for placement.

9 Sew yellow buttons centered on the fuchsia flowers, and bright pink buttons on the orange flowers.

Geometrics Mantle Scarf

size: 41" x 15½"

materials

1 yd green stripe fabric
½ yd fuchsia tonal print fabric
⅔ yd cotton batting

4 large lime green buttons
Coordinating sewing threads
Monofilament invisible thread

cutting

Cut 1 piece 41½" x 11", 8 of piece A (note that pattern is to be placed on fold), 8 of piece B. This fabric will also be used for back.

Cut 8 of piece C from fuchsia fabric.

construction

1 See patterns on pages 110 and 111. Lay two of piece A (rst), and pin to batting. Cut batting out and sew together. Leave the bottom flat edge open. Repeat with remaining A pieces. Trim seams; turn and press.

2 Pin B pieces (rst) and stitch. Repeat with C pieces. Leave bottom flat edges open. The bottom of the triangle is the longest edge. Trim seams and points; turn and press.

3 Topstitch ¼" from sewn edges of the A dimensional units. Center the fuchsia triangles (C pieces) on top of the A units and pin, then stitch together, stitching the triangle ¼" from the sewn edges. Stack the B units on top of the triangles and pin, then stitch together, stitching the B unit ¼" from the sewn edge. Sew across the open edges, stitching through all layers.

4 Lay the stacked units (rst) on the 41½" x 11" green piece. Spread units evenly across one edge, aligning the straight edges of the units to the edge of the strip. Pin.

5 Lay the backing fabric right side up on the batting. Lay the top right side down on top of the backing so that the backing and top are (rst). The stacked dimensional units will be between the top and backing. Pin and cut out the backing and batting. Stitch together, leaving a 4" opening along the bottom edge. Trim corners and seams. Turn right side out, press, and whipstitch the opening closed.

6 Quilt ¼" around the inside edge of the long strip. Sew buttons to the center of the triangle points. Place on mantle so that the dimensional flaps hang down in front of the mantle.

Crazy Footstool

size: 11" x 15"

materials

⅔ yd green tie dyed/batik fabric

Scraps yellow tonal print

Scraps fuchsia tonal print

Scraps dark green tonal print

Scraps orange tonal print

DMC 6 strand cotton embroidery floss in the following colors: 726 (yellow), 911 (green), 907 (bright green), 720 (orange), 3607 (fuchsia) and 3609 (pink)

Footstool

Heavy duty stapler

Assorted yellow, orange, lime green, dark green, and dark rose buttons

Coordinated sewing threads

✂ cutting

Cut the base cover of the footstool from the green tie dyed/batik fabric. Measure the footstool width and length including the sides to the base where the fabric will turn under. Add 8" each to the width and the length for your cutting size.

Cut 1 of D and 2 of A (reverse 1 of the pieces) from the yellow fabric

Cut 1 of B and 2 of C (reverse 1 of the pieces) from the green fabric

Cut 1 of A and 2 of D (reverse 1 of the pieces) from the fuchsia fabric

Cut 1 of C and 2 of B (reverse 1 of the pieces) from the orange fabric

construction

1 See patterns on pages 112 and 113. The pattern pieces are arranged on the pattern page like they will be stitched to each other. The embroidery stitch and button placement is also shown for the block unit. Additional blocks with stitches are shown for the blocks that surround the combined block.

2 Sew the pieces that were cut in 1 piece (A, B, C., and D) together for the center block. See above and pattern for the sewing edges. Sew A and B together, then sew C across the A/B end. Sew D to the A/C edge.

3 Pin the block right sides together (rst) with one of the fabrics for the block back and cut out the back. Pin these two pieces (rst) to the batting. Cut batting out and sew together. Lay the 2 A pieces (rst) and pin to batting. Cut batting out and sew together. Repeat with remaining B, C, and D pieces. Trim seams and corners. Cut a 1" slit in the batting and the next layer of fabric; turn right side out and press seams. Whipstitch the opening closed.

4 Pin the block centered onto the tie-dyed block. Arrange the A, B, C and D units around the block and pin. See the photograph for placement. The embroidery floss is divisible into six strands. Use three strands for the stitching. Stitch the pieces to the background around the edges using the feather, cretan, blanket, and herringbone stitches. Stitch over the seams of the block. Stitch the embroidery flowers and leaves on the pieces as indicated on the patterns. Sew on buttons.

5 Remove the screws from the legs of the footstool. Center the cover on top of the footstool and pull sides of the cover to the back. Tuck corners. Staple edges to the back of the footstool and screw legs on.

for the baby

chapter 6

for the baby

PROJECTS

Love Memory Album

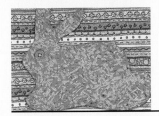

Lucky Ducky Chairback

On the Farm Wall Hanging

Stripes Crib Quilt

Love Memory Album

size: 11" x 12"
Size will vary depending on album used.

materials

½ yd purple, lime green, and blue plaid flannel
¼ yd lime green marbled flannel
Scraps turquoise marbled flannel
Scraps fuchsia marbled flannel
½ yd muslin

½ yd cotton batting
Photo album
Coordinating sewing threads
Monofilament invisible thread

✂ cutting

Cut 2 pieces 5½" x 7" and 1½" border strips from the lime green fabric.

Cut 2 of the B heart piece from the fuchsia fabric.

Cut 8 of the A triangle piece from the turquoise fabric.

Cut 1 piece 11¼" x 22¾" for the album cover and 2 inside pocket pieces 12½" x 4" from the plaid fabric. For different sized albums, measure the height and width and subtract ¼" from this size for the cover. For the pockets, cut 4" x the album height plus ½".

construction

1 See pattern on page 115. Lay the two heart pieces right sides together (rst) and pin to batting. Cut batting out and sew together. Repeat with remaining A triangle pieces and with the two lime green rectangles. Trim seams and points and clip inside points. Cut a 1" slit in the batting and the next layer of fabric. Turn right side out and press seams. Whipstitch the opening closed.

2 Sew the green border strips to the top edges and bottom edges and then to the side edges of the plaid cover.

3 Fold a double ¼" hem on one long edge of each pocket piece and stitch. Pin the pockets, (rst), on each side edge of the album cover, matching the long edge of the pocket without the hem to the side edge.

4 Lay the muslin fabric on the batting. Lay the album cover right side down on top of the muslin so that the muslin and top are (rst) on the batting. Pin and cut out the muslin and batting. The pockets will be pinned between the top and the muslin. Stitch together, leaving a 4" opening along the bottom edge. Trim corners and seams. Turn, press, and whipstitch the opening closed.

5 Center the heart on the lime green rectangle and pin. Stitch together by stitching the heart ¼" from the edge. Place this rectangle and heart unit centered on the front of the album cover and pin. You will have to wrap the cover around the album to find the center front. Stitch to the album cover stitching ¼" from the rectangle edge.

6 Place triangles to cover the corners of the rectangles with the long flat edge over the rectangle. See the photograph for placement. Space the triangles so that the two shorter edges are ⅓" away from the rectangle. Pin and stitch ¼" from these two edges.

7 Slide pockets over the side edges of the album.

Lucky Ducky Chairback

size: 14" x 12½"

materials

½ yd wavy stripe fabric
⅛ yd lime green dot fabric
⅓ yd turquoise fabric
½ yd yellow dot fabric
Scraps orange tonal fabric

1 turquoise button
½ yd cotton batting
Coordinating sewing threads
Monofilament invisible thread

✁ cutting

Cut 2 of piece A (with 1 piece reversed), and 4 strips 2½" x 23" for the ties from the yellow dot fabric.

Cut 2 of piece B (with 1 piece reversed) from orange tonal fabric.

Cut 9½" x 8½" block from turquoise fabric.

Cut 1½" wide inner border strips from lime green dot fabric.

Cut 2½" wide outer border strips from the wavy stripe fabric. Cut so that the stripes on the side border strips run in the same direction as the top and bottom border strips.

construction

1 See pattern on page 116. Layer two of piece B (beak) right sides together (rst) and pin to batting. Cut batting out and sew together, leaving the straighter edge open. Trim seams, turn, and press.

2 Place the two duck pieces (rst). Insert the beak between the two duck pieces, aligning the open edge of the beak with the front edge of the head. The beak will be sandwiched between the two fabrics. Pin to batting. Cut batting out, and sew together all the way around. Trim seams and cut inside curves. Cut a 2" slit in the batting and the next layer of fabric, and turn right side out. Press seams. Whipstitch the opening closed.

3 Sew a lime green border strip to each side of the turquoise block, then to the top and bottom edges. Repeat by sewing the outer border strips to the sides then to the top and bottom edges.

4 Center the duck on the turquoise fabric and pin in place. Secure by stitching tacking stitches from the back of the block, sewing through the bottom layer of the duck. Sew the button on for the eye, stitching through all layers.

5 Fold the yellow tie strips in half lengthwise. Stitch together on the open edge and on one end. Turn and press.

6 Lay the backing fabric right side up on top of the batting. Pin two each of the unstitched ends of the ties to the top left and right edges. Align so that the ends and the sides match. See the illustration on page 37, for Apples of My Eye Chairback. Lay the top right side down on top of the backing so that the backing and top are (rst) with the ties between them. Pin, and cut out the backing and batting. Stitch together, leaving a 4" opening along the bottom edge. Trim corners and seams. Turn, press, and whipstitch the opening closed.

On the Farm Wall Hanging

size: 26" x 20½"

materials

¼ yd green tonal print
1 yd large print fabric
⅓ yd stripe print fabric
¼ yd light turquoise print fabric
¼ yd yellow print fabric
¼ yd yellow marbled fabric
¼ yd orange tonal print fabric
¼ yd pink tonal fabric

⅔ yd cotton batting
DMC 6 strand cotton embroidery floss, color 911
2 turquoise buttons
3 orange buttons
1 yellow button
1 light turquoise button
Coordinating sewing threads
Monofilament invisible thread

cutting

Cut 1 piece 9½" x 7½" (A) and 1 piece, 9½" x 8½" (D) from the stripe fabric.

Cut 1 piece 14½" x 7½" (E) and 1 piece, 7½" x 6½" (B) from the light turquoise print fabric.

Cut 1 piece 5½" x 8½" (C) from the yellow print fabric.

Cut 2½" wide outer border strips from the large print fabric. (will also be used for the back).

Cut 2 of the moon (with 1 piece reversed) and 4

of the beak (with 2 pieces reversed) from the yellow fabric.

Cut 2 of the bunny (with 1 piece reversed) and 2 of the heart from the pink tonal fabric.

Cut 4 of the ducky (with 2 pieces reversed) and 2 of the carrot (with 1 piece reversed) from the orange tonal fabric.

Cut 2 of the carrot top (with 1 piece reversed) and 1¾" wide inner border strips from the green fabric.

construction

1 See patterns on pages 117, 118, and 119. See the illustration for placement of blocks. Sew block A to block B. Sew block C to block D. Sew block E to the top of the C/D unit. Sew the A/B unit to the E/C/D unit.

2 Sew green border strips to the side edges of the block unit, then green strips to the top and bottom edges. Repeat by sewing the large print border strips to the side edges, then to the top and bottom edges.

3 Lay the two beak pieces right sides together (rst) and pin to batting. Repeat with the carrot top. Cut batting out and sew together, leaving the short edge of the beak and the bottom edge of the carrot top open. Trim seams and points and clip inside points. Turn right side out and press.

4 Lay the two moon pieces (rst), and pin to batting. Repeat with bunny, heart, ducky, and carrot pieces. Cut the batting out. Insert the beak between the two ducky fabric pieces, aligning the open edge of the beak with the front edge of the

head, so that the beak is sandwiched between the two fabrics. Sew all pieces. Trim seams and corners and clip inside curves and points. Cut a 1" slit in the top layer of fabric. Turn right side out and press seams. Whipstitch the opening closed.

5 Pin the moon to block A, the two duckies to block E, the heart to block B, the bunny to block D and the carrot to block C. Center them on the blocks and pin. Tuck the carrot top bottom edge ¼" under the carrot. Stitch to the blocks stitching ⅛" from the edge.

6 See photograph for placement of buttons. Sew three orange buttons hanging from the moon. Use three strands of green embroidery floss to stitch long, straight stitches to attach the buttons to the top point of the moon. Sew one yellow button at the point on the heart. Sew a light turquoise button for the eye on the bunny, and sew a turquoise button for the eye on each ducky.

7 Lay the backing fabric right side up on the batting. Lay the quilt top right side down on top of the backing so that the backing and top are (rst). Pin and cut out the backing and batting. Stitch together leaving a 4" opening along the bottom edge. Trim corners and seams. Turn right side out, press, and whipstitch the opening closed.

8 Quilt ¼" around the edges of the carrot, heart, moon, bunny, duckies, the block seams, the border seams, and along the edge of the quilt.

Stripes Crib Quilt

size: 34" x 48"

materials

Select 1 yd each of 6 coordinating flannel prints
1½ yds cotton batting
Coordinating sewing threads
Monofilament sewing threads

cutting

The best way to cut the strips and to coordinate the colors is to lay them together. Also, choose the fabric for the dimensional pieces as you coordinate the stripes. Work with two or three rows at a time, starting with row A, B, C, etc. Cut the strips according to the dimensions on the illustration. Lay them in place as you cut them and then choose the next rows. Cut the dimensional pieces at the same time, and lay them on top of the strip that they will be sewed to.

Cut 6 of piece 1 for column A, 8 of piece 2 for column A, 8 of piece 3 for column D, 6 of piece 4 for the middle of column E, 10 of piece 5 for column H, and 4 of piece 1 for column H.

construction

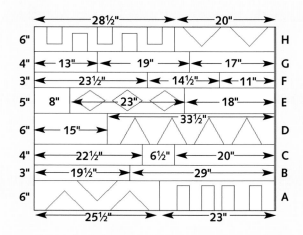

1 See patterns on pages 120, 121, and 122. Lay two of piece 1 right sides together (rst) and pin to batting. Repeat with remaining pieces of 1 and with 2, 3, 4, and 5 pieces. Cut batting out and sew together. Leave the edges that will be sewn into the seams unstitched. Trim seams and corners; turn right side out and press. For piece 4, sew together around the entire piece. Cut a 1" slit in the batting and the next layer of fabric, and turn right side out and press seams. Whipstitch the opening closed.

2 Sew together the strips of each column, sewing the end seams (rst). Start with column A. Lay each column back in place when you finish sewing and pick up the next column. This will ensure that you keep the columns in the order you selected them. Also, it will help to put a pin in the ends on one side to mark them so that you do not turn the columns the wrong direction.

3 Sew the columns together at the side seams, starting with rows A and B. As you reach a seam that will have dimensional pieces sewn in, arrange the dimensional units on one of the strips. Space them evenly and pin in place with the open edges aligned with the edge of the strip. Sew the two strips right sides together with the dimensional pieces sandwiched between them.

4 Sew the dimensional units that are on the outside seams of column A and H to the edges of the columns. Evenly space the four diamond pieces on column E. Topstitch in place ¼" from the edge.

5 Stitch all the dimensional pieces to the background by stitching ¼" from the edge, sewing around the dimensional piece.

6 Cut the quilt back and the batting 1" larger than the quilt top all the way around (see "Getting Started" on page 14). Quilt ¼" around the seams and the dimensional pieces.

7 Sew on binding (see "Getting Started" on page 15). Press.

chapter 7

it's Christmas

it's Christmas

PROJECTS

Merry Christmas Tree Skirt

Christmas Trees Wall Hanging

Stars Table Runner

Merry Christmas Tree Skirt

size: 43" x 43"

materials

1½ yds green and white stripe fabric
1½ yds muslin
1 yd red marbled print
⅔ yd green marbled print
1½ yds cotton batting

16 red buttons
8 green buttons
Coordinating sewing threads
Monofilament invisible thread

✂ cutting

Cut 16 of piece B and 8 of piece A from green and white stripe fabric (note that piece A requires that the fabric be cut on the fold).

Cut 16 of piece C and 16 of piece E from the red fabric.

Cut 16 of piece D and 1½" binding strip for the opening around the tree from the green fabric.

⚘ construction

1 See patterns on pages 125 and 126. Lay two of piece B right sides together (rst) and pin to batting. Cut batting out and sew together leaving the bottom edge unstitched. Repeat with remaining B pieces and with the E pieces. Trim seams and points. Turn right side out, and press.

2 Pin two of piece C (rst). Repeat with remaining C pieces and with the D pieces. Sew together, leaving the bottom edge unstitched. Trim seams and points; turn and press.

3 Place a C unit on top of a B unit, align, and center on the open edges. Place the D unit on top of the B unit, again aligned and centered on the bottom open edges. See the photograph for placement. Stitch across the open ends to join together.

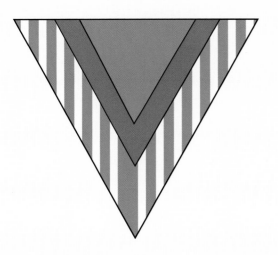

4 Sew the A pieces together along the side edges. Leave two of the edges unstitched for the opening.

5 Pin a triangle unit (rst) to the bottom edge of each piece A section. Align edges.

6 Lay the muslin fabric for the back on the batting. Lay the quilt top right side down on top of the muslin so that the muslin and top are (rst). The triangle units will be sandwiched between the top and the muslin. Pin and cut out the muslin and batting. Stitch together leaving the top circular edge unstitched. Trim corners and seams. Turn right side out and press.

7 Quilt ¼" around the seams.

8 Pin the E pieces to the top open edge, aligning the open ends to the edge of each A piece. Sew in place along the open edge. Sew binding around the top edge, folding ends under and covering the edges of the E pieces. (See "Getting Started" on page 15.)

9 Sew buttons at the points, sewing red buttons on the green points and green buttons on the red points.

Christmas Trees Wall Hanging

size: 24½" x 30"

materials

2 yds red tonal print

½ yd metallic red plaid fabric

¼ yd green fabric with metallic gold print

⅓ yd of a 2nd green fabric with metallic gold print

½ yd of a 3rd green fabric with metallic gold print

1 yd cotton batting

4 – 1" gold star buttons

Coordinating sewing threads

Monofilament invisible thread

✂ cutting

Cut 4 blocks 7" x 10" and 2½" wide border strips from the red tonal print. This fabric will also be used for the back.

Cut sashing strips 3" wide from the red plaid fabric.

Cut corner blocks 3" x 3" from the 2nd green fabric (the one requiring ⅓ yd).

Cut 1½ wide binding strips from the 3rd green fabric (the one requiring ½ yd).

Cut 4 of piece A from one of the green fabrics, and 2 of piece A from each of the other two green fabrics.

Cut 4 of piece B from one of the green fabrics and 6 of piece B from each of the other two green fabrics.

↗ construction

1 See patern on page 123. Join two red blocks together with sashing strips to the top and bottom edges of the blocks. Sew strips on the top and bottom ends of the block unit. Repeat with remaining two blocks. Join two sashings together at the ends with corner blocks, and add corner blocks on each end. Repeat to form three units. Join the block units together with one of these sashing strips. Sew a sashing strip on each side of this completed unit. (See the illustration on page 21, for the "Morning Star Quilt.")

2 Sew border strips to the top and bottom edges then sew to the side edges.

3 Lay two of piece A right sides together (rst) and pin to batting. Cut batting out and sew together. Repeat with remaining A pieces and with the B pieces. Trim seams and corners. Cut a 1" slit in the batting and the next layer of fabric, turn right side out and press seams. Whipstitch the opening closed. Repeat with the C pieces, but leave one end unstitched. Turn through the opening and press.

4 The trees are constructed of one piece A dimensional unit and two piece B dimensional units. They were cut from varying green fabrics, and these units should be mixed in forming the trees so that they have each of the three green fabrics in each tree. Arrange dimensional tree pieces, centered on each block, to form each tree.

5 Pin the largest tree unit (A), centered 1" below the top edge of the red block. Pin a B unit on each side of the A unit, so that the A unit overlaps the top point of the B units. See the photograph for placement. Whipstitch the tree pieces to the block, stitching the top side edges only. Leave the bottom side edges unstitched.

6 Pin the tree trunk (C) so that the unstitched end is ¼" under the tree. Whipstitch to the block all the way around.

7 Cut the quilt back and the batting 1" larger than the quilt top all the way around (see "Getting Started" on page 14). Quilt ¼" around the trees and along the seams.

8 Sew on binding (see "Getting Started" on page 15). Press.

9 Sew a gold star button at the top of each tree.

Stars Table Runner

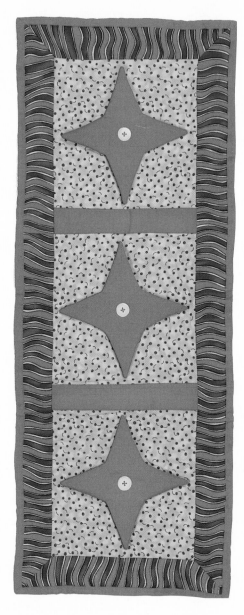

size: 12½" x 32"

Length can be increased by adding one or more blocks.

materials

1½ yds red fabric
⅓ yd lime green print fabric
⅓ yd wavy stripe fabric
½ yd cotton batting

3 large yellow buttons
Coordinating sewing threads
Monofilament invisible thread

✂ cutting

Cut 6 of the star pieces, 2" wide sashing strips and 1½" wide border strips from the red fabric. Use this fabric also for the back.

Cut 3 squares 9" x 9" from the lime green fabric.
Cut 2½" wide border strips from the stripe fabric.

⚮ construction

1 See pattern on page 124. Lay two of the star pieces right sides together and pin to batting. Cut batting out and sew together. Repeat with remaining star pieces. Trim seams and points. Clip inside curves. Cut a 1" slit in the batting and the next layer of fabric, and turn right side out. Press seams. Whipstitch the opening closed.

2 Join lime green blocks with red sashing strips.

3 You can stitch the borders the same as the other projects. However, if you are sewing a stripe border, miter the corners for a better appearance of the stripes. To miter the corners, cut border strips so that they are 7" longer than the quilt edges. Pin border strips to the top and bottom edges, leaving an excess border of equal length on each end. Start, and stop, stitching ¼" from ends of the quilt. Repeat by sewing on the side border strips, also starting and stopping ¼" from each end and leaving excess border on each end. Overlap the excess border strips at each corner. Fold one end strip under (rst) at a 45 degree angle and press this angle. Pin the borders together, and stitch on the fold line. Trim seams. Repeat for each corner.

4 Attach the stars, centered on the lime green blocks, by sewing yellow buttons to the center of the stars going through all layers.

5 Cut the quilt back and the batting 1" larger than the quilt top all the way around. Stipple quilt the lime green block around the stars (see "Getting Started" on page 14).

6 Sew on binding (see "Getting Started" on page 15). Press.

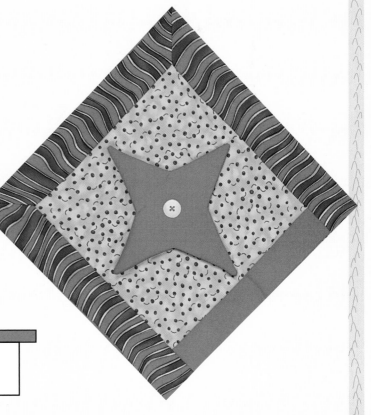

Mitering the borders. A. Stitch with excess ends and lay one across the other. B. With right sides together, fold one end under at a 45 degree angle. Press the fold, pin, then stitch together on the fold line.

chapter 8

Lazy Daisy and Lazy Daisy Flower

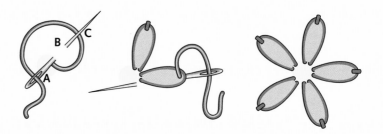

Come up at A and go back down close to A. Come back up at B with the floss forming a loop behind the needle. Go back down at C, stitching over the loop. Make a flower by stitching five or six lazy daisy stitches in a circle.

Colonial Knot

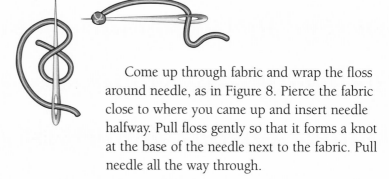

Come up through fabric and wrap the floss around needle, as in Figure 8. Pierce the fabric close to where you came up and insert needle halfway. Pull floss gently so that it forms a knot at the base of the needle next to the fabric. Pull needle all the way through.

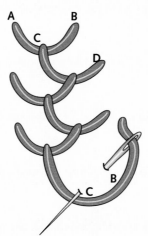

Feather Stitch

Come up at A and go down at B, leaving the floss loose. Come back up at C, behind the floss and pull to form a loop. Go back down at D to repeat stitch. Continue with stitches. Stitches can be varied by stitching two to the right and two to the left.

embroidery stitches

Herringbone Stitch

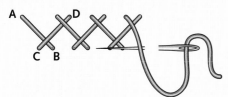

Come up at A and go down at B. Come back up at C and go down at D. Repeat.

Cretan Stitch

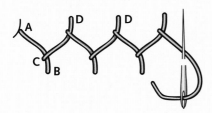

Come up at A and go down at B. Come up at C behind the floss and go down at D. Repeat.

Blanket Stitch

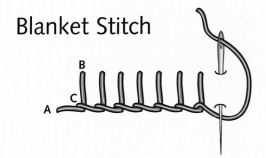

Come up at A and go down at B. Come up at C behind the floss. Repeat.

Straight Stitch

Come up at A and go down at B to form a single straight stitch. These can be stitched in lines to outline an area, or can be stitched radiating out from a point in a circle to form a flower.

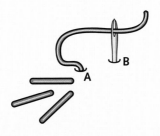

Patterns

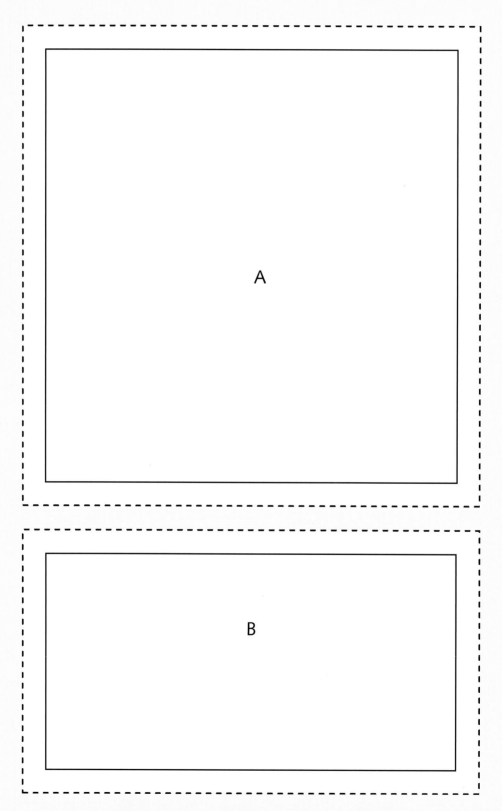

A

B

Morning Stars Wall Hanging

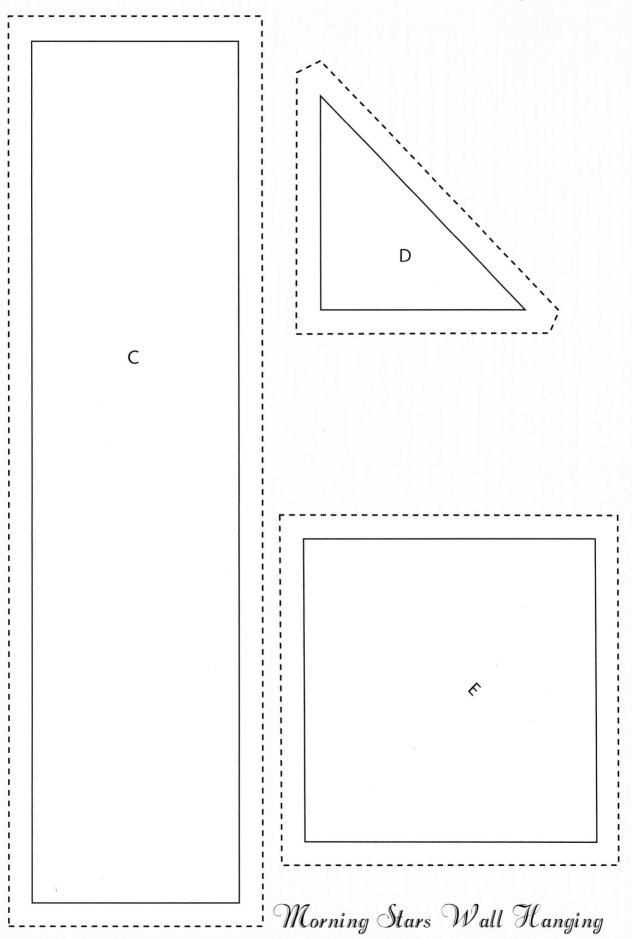

C

D

E

Morning Stars Wall Hanging

Hearts to You Wall Hanging

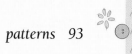

Flying in Circles

A

B

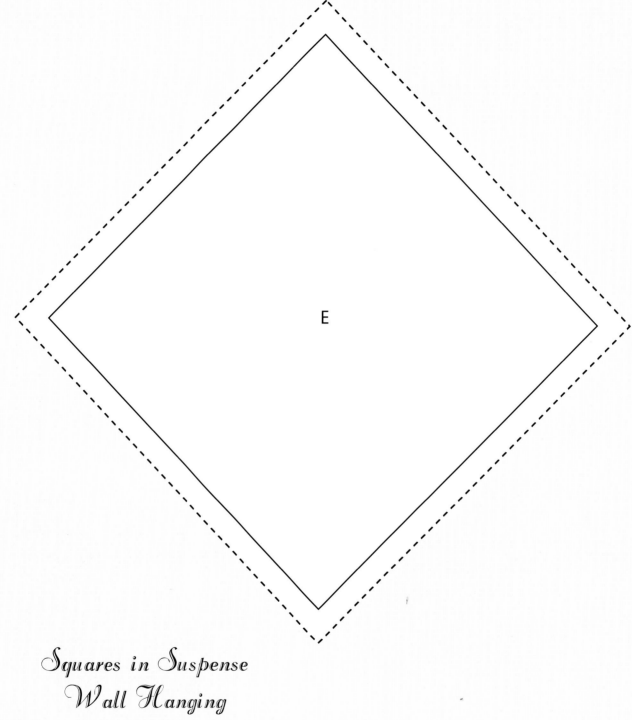

E

Squares in Suspense
Wall Hanging

D

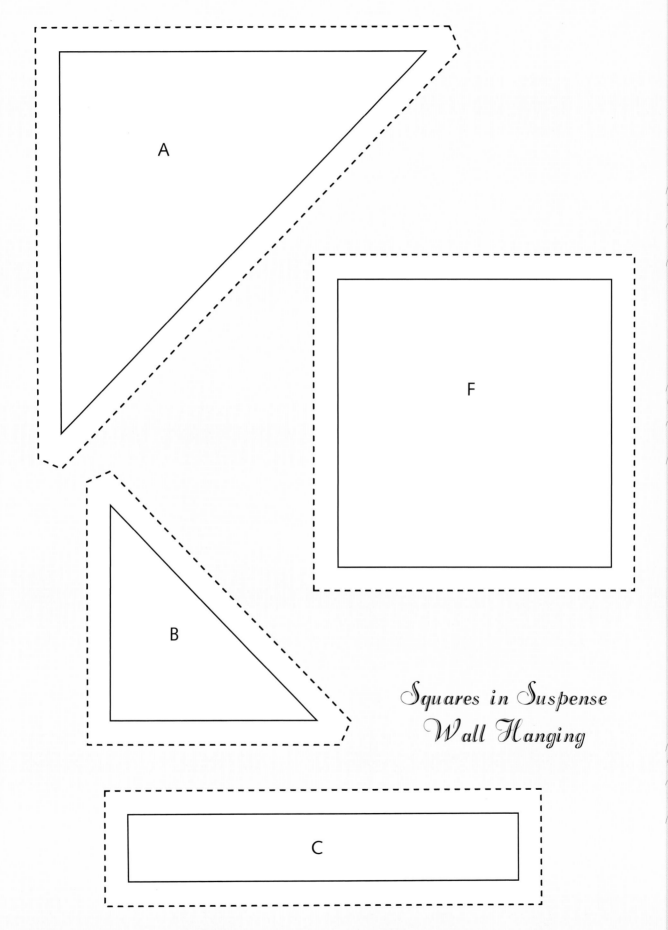

A

F

B

Squares in Suspense
Wall Hanging

C

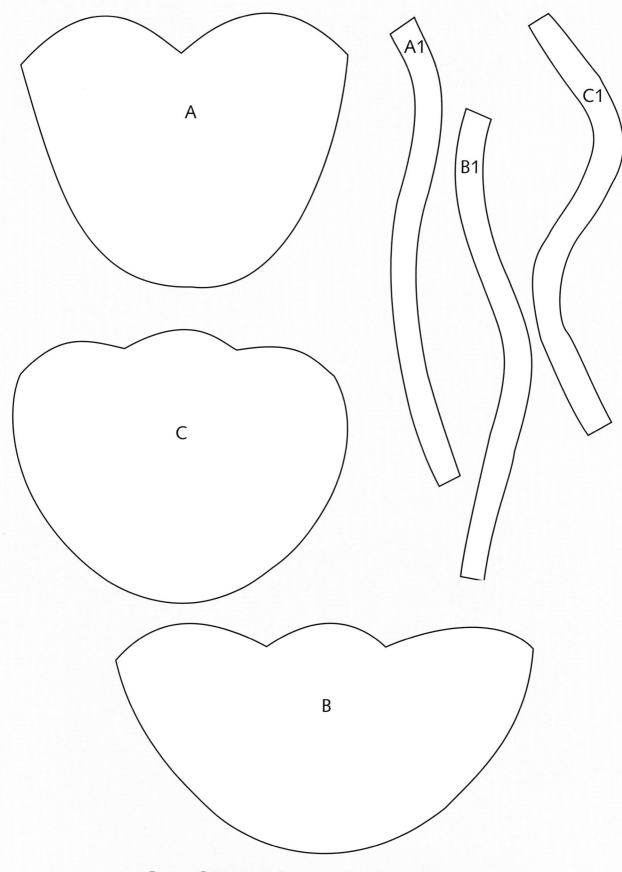

A

A1

C1

B1

C

B

Let's Bloom Panel Wall Hanging

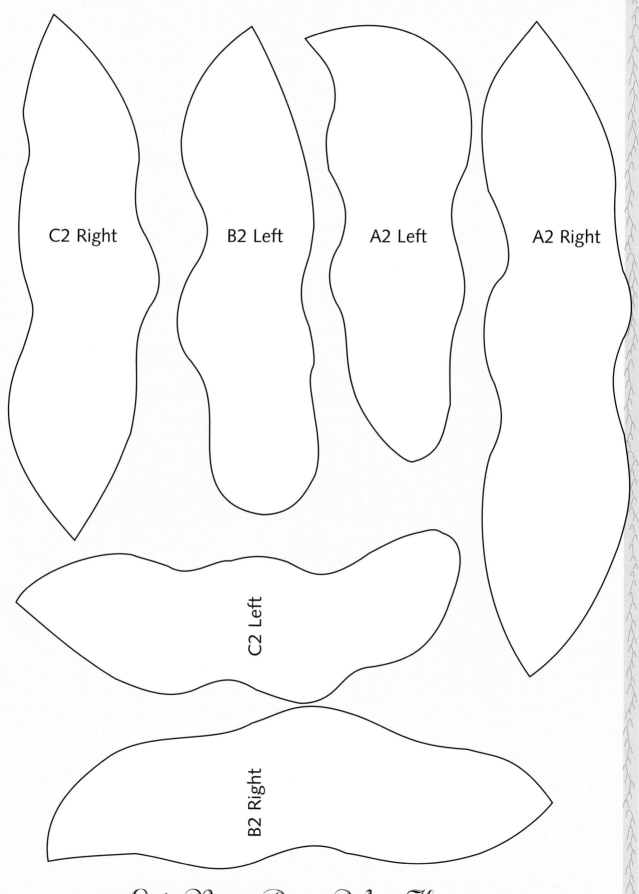

C2 Right

B2 Left

A2 Left

A2 Right

C2 Left

B2 Right

Let's Bloom Panel Wall Hanging

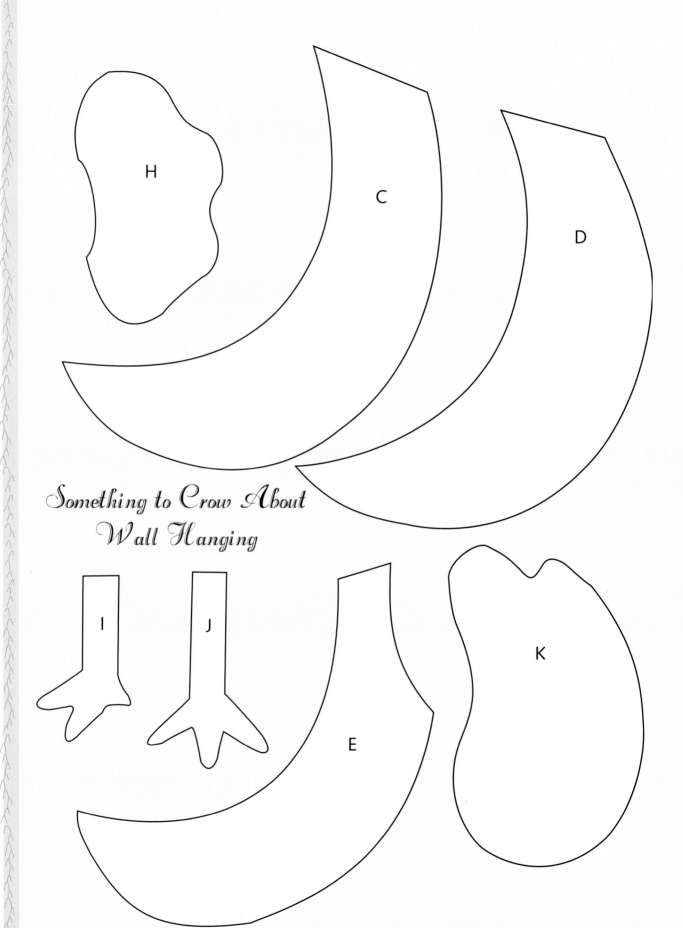

Something to Crow About
Wall Hanging

F

B

G

*Something to Crow
About Wall Hanging*

A

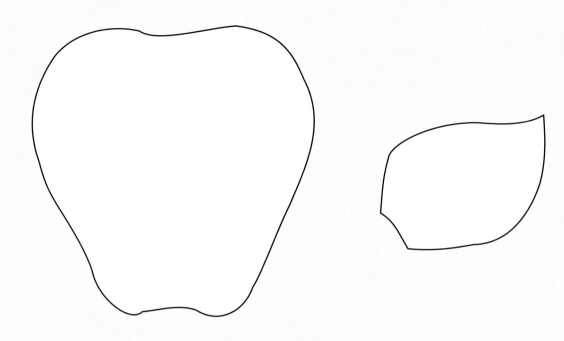

Apples of My Eye Chairback

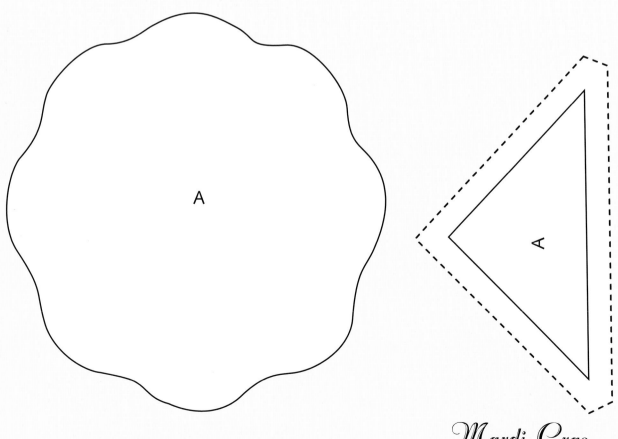

A

Puff Flowers Chair Panel

A

*Mardi Gras
Place Mat*

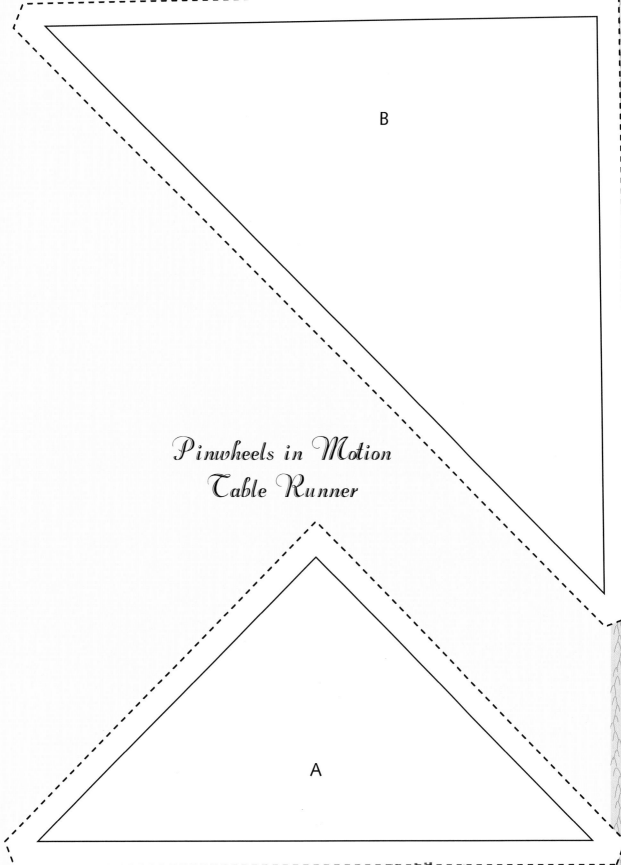

Pinwheels in Motion
Table Runner

B

A

Hamilton East Public Library

Vegetable Patch Centerpiece

A

Vegetable
Patch
Centerpiece

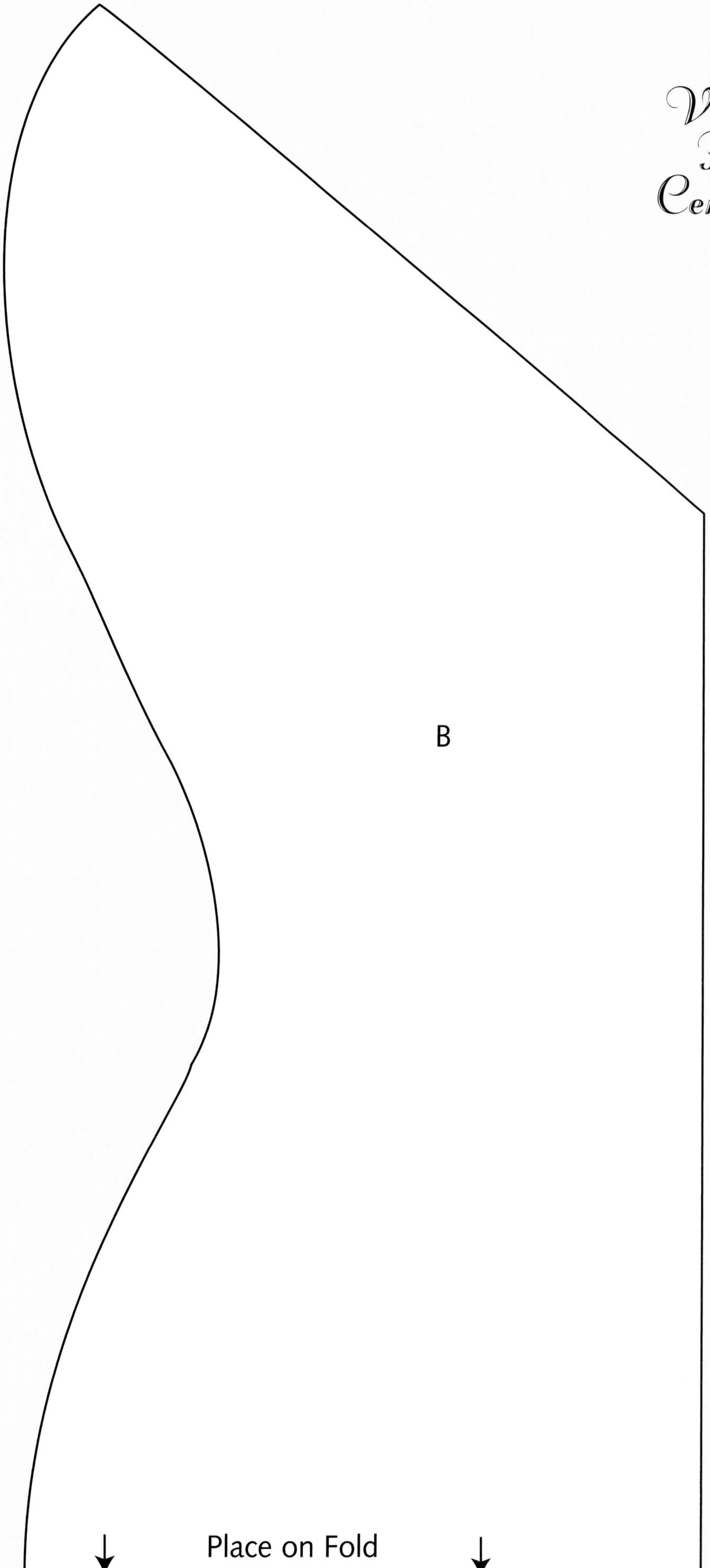

B

↓   Place on Fold   ↓

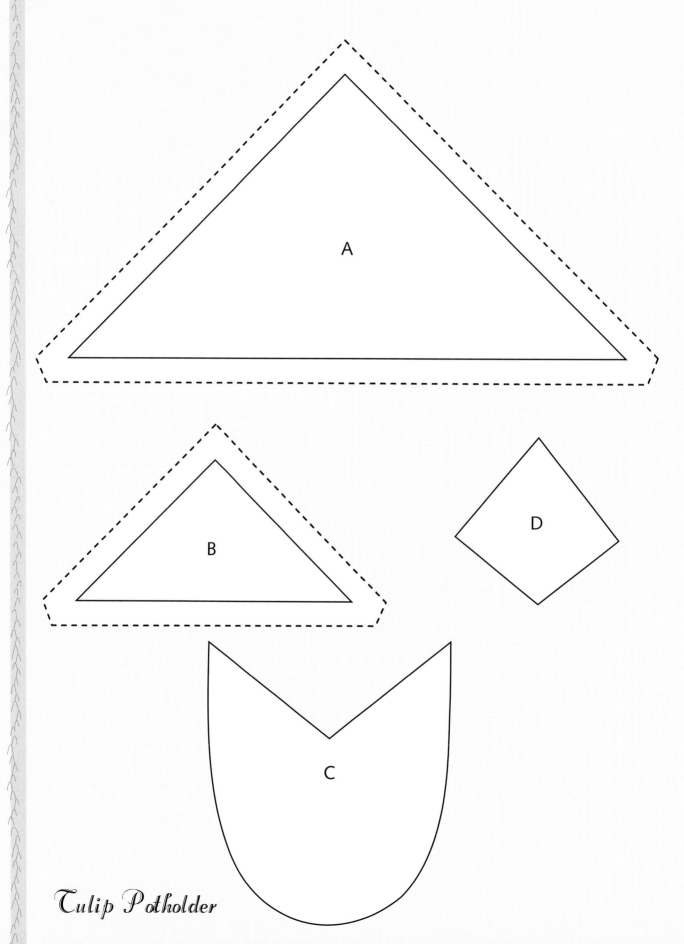

Tulip Potholder

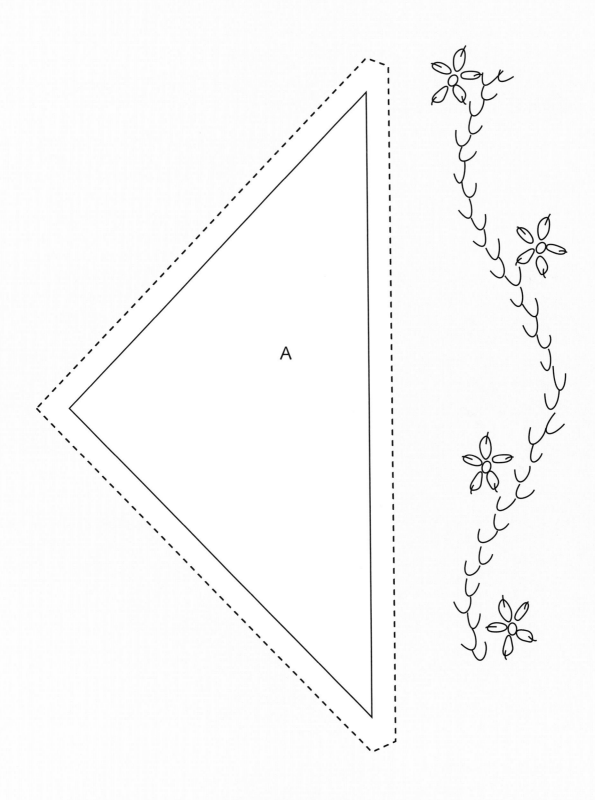

Spring Flowers Table Runner

A Single Blossom
Pillow

B

Place on Fold

A

Diamond and Squares
Buffet Scarf

A

B

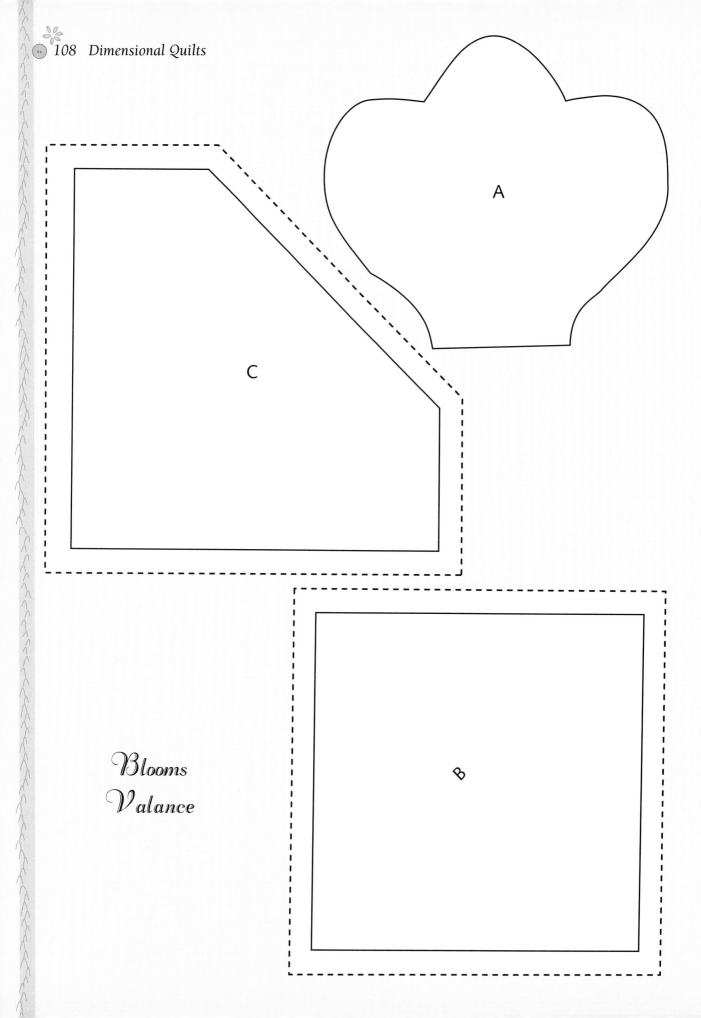

Blooms
Valance

A

C

B

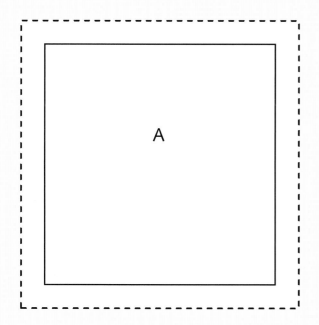

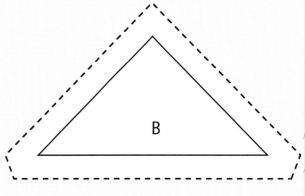

Let's Play Picnic Basket

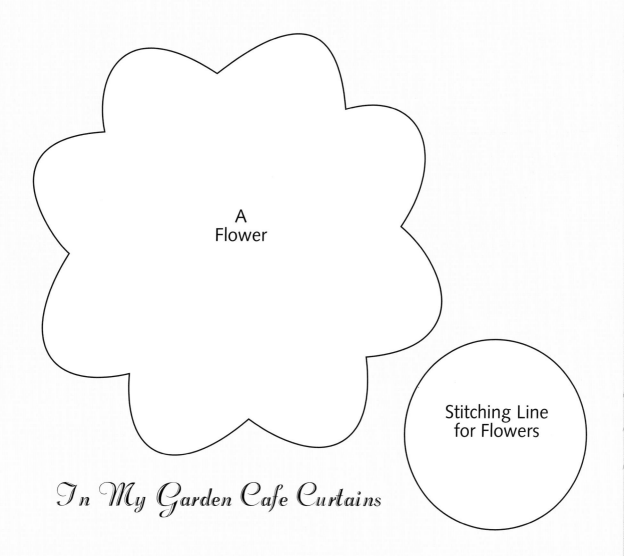

A
Flower

Stitching Line
for Flowers

In My Garden Cafe Curtains

Geometrics
Mantle Scarf

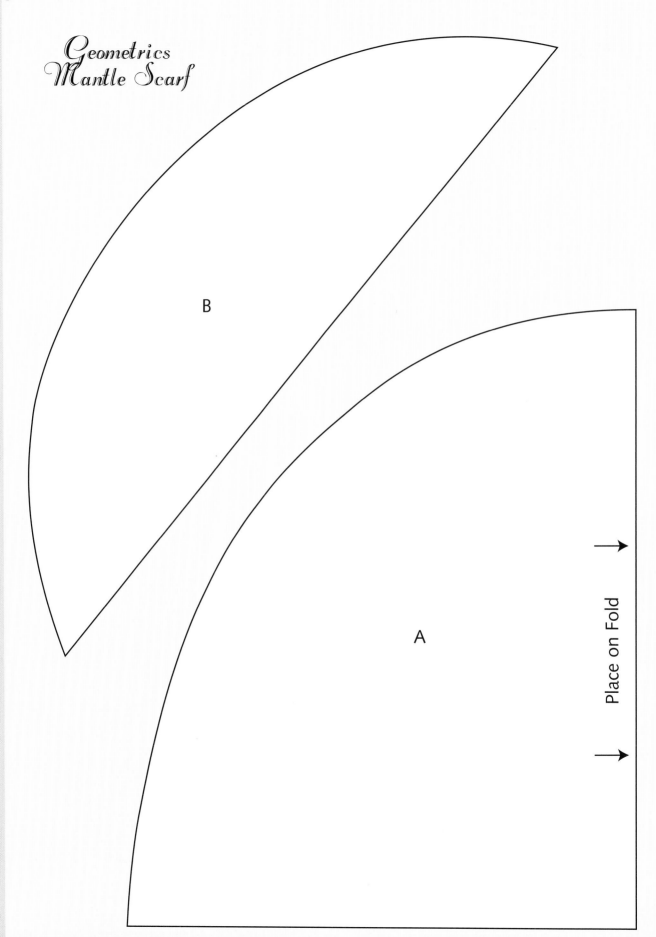

B

A

Place on Fold

C

Geometrics
Mantle Scarf

Crazy Footstool

Crazy Footstool

1

2

3

Pattern is 50%.
Photocopy at 200%.

Pattern is 50%.
Photocopy at 200%.

Pattern is 50%.
Photocopy at 200%.

Ocean Waves Pillow

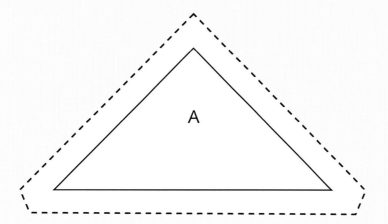

A

B
Heart

Love Memory Album

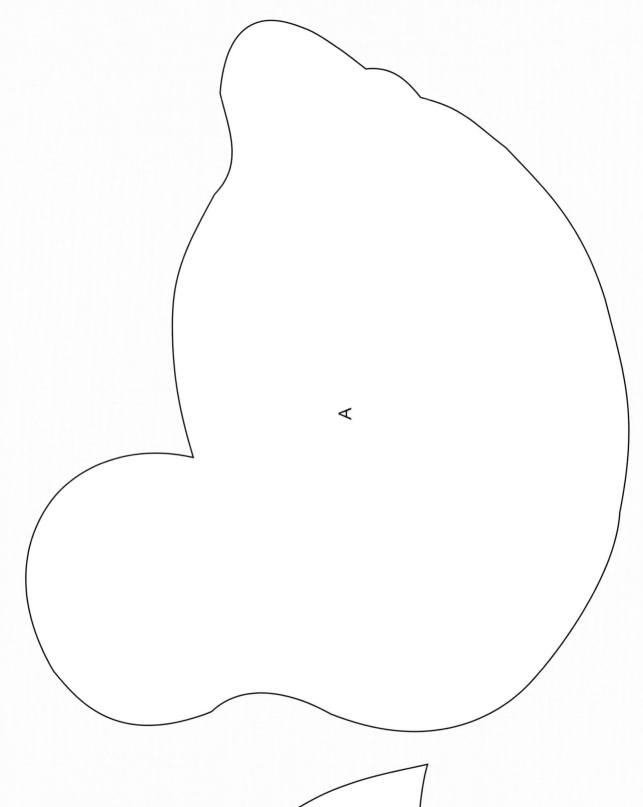

A

B

Lucky Ducky
Chairback

On the Farm
Wall Hanging

Carrot

Carrot
Top

Bunny

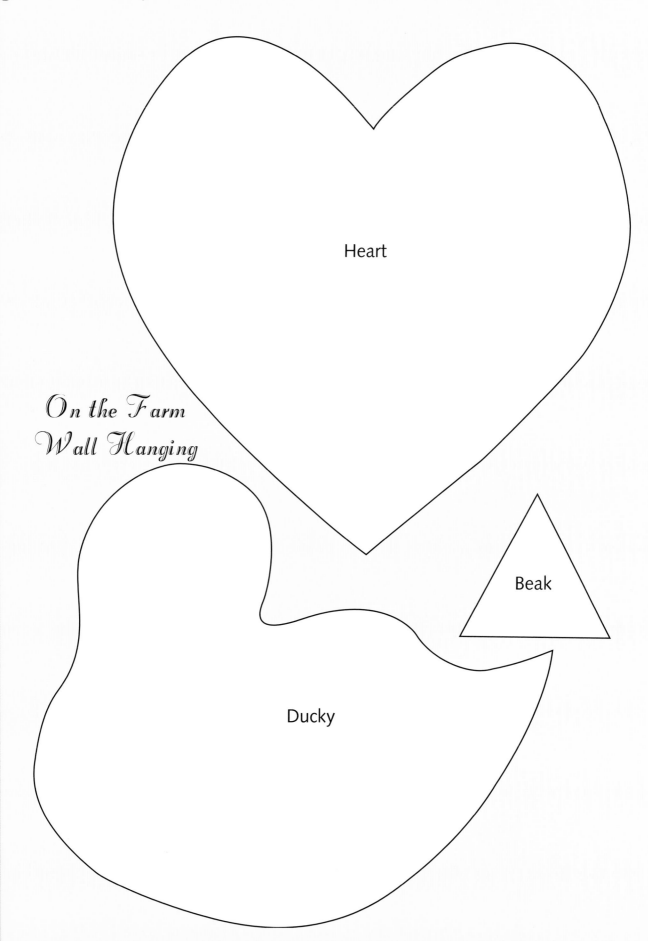

Heart

*On the Farm
Wall Hanging*

Beak

Ducky

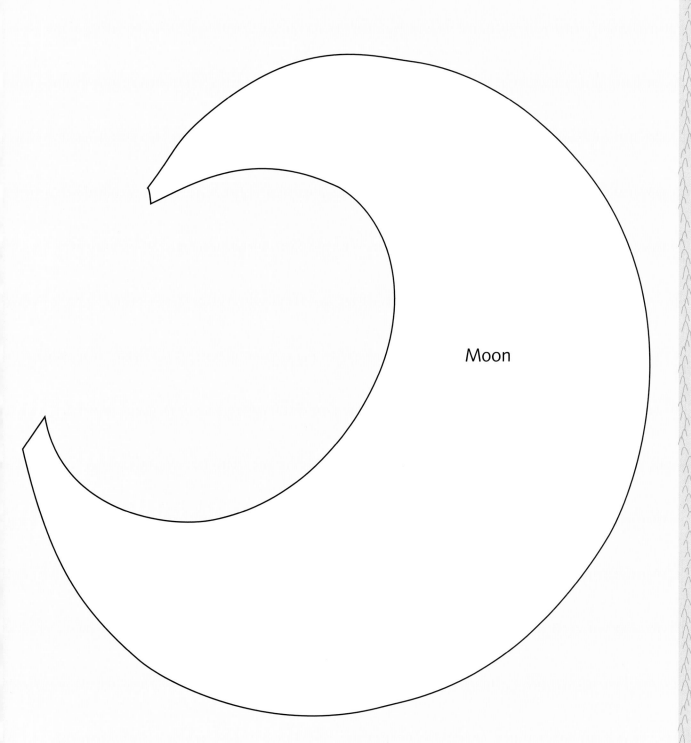

Moon

On the Farm Wall
Hanging

Stripes Crib Quilt

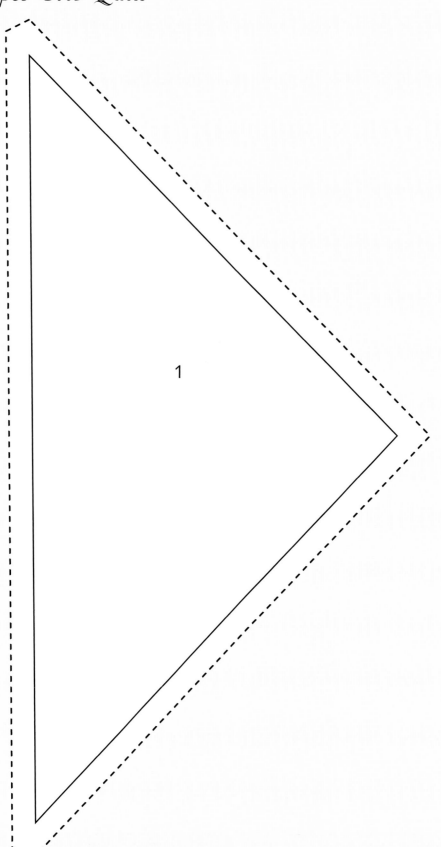

1

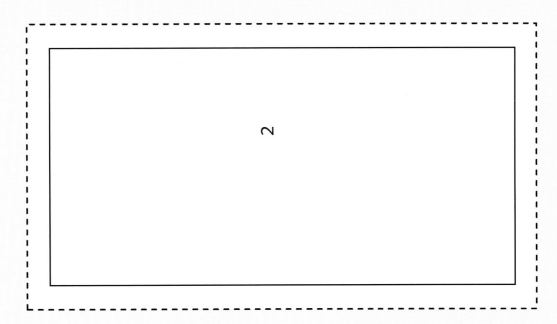

2

Stripes Crib Quilt

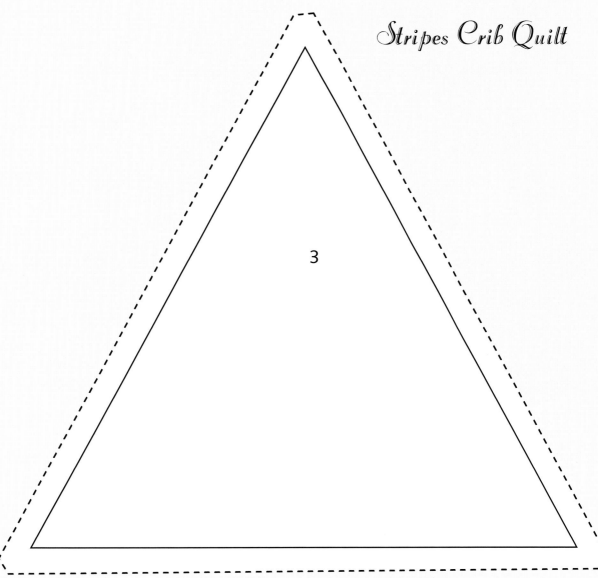

3

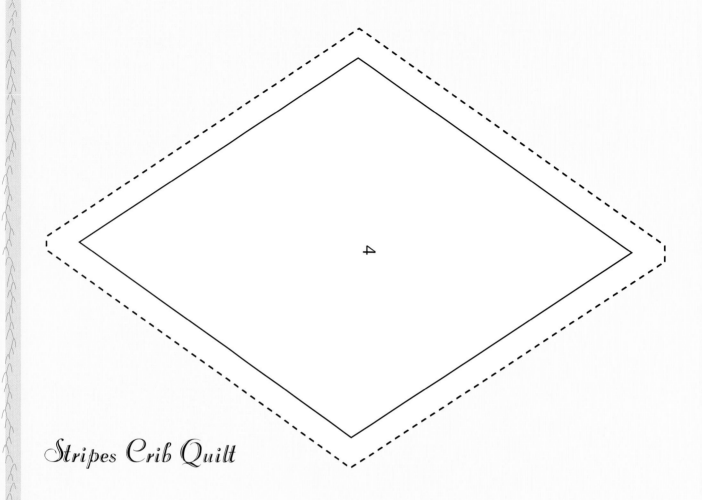

4

Stripes Crib Quilt

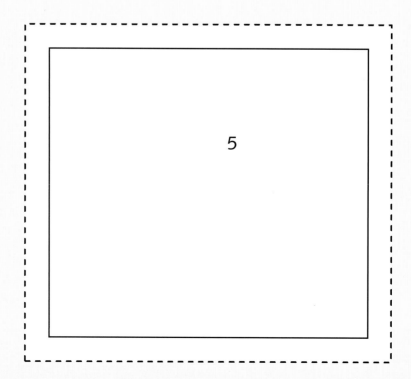

5

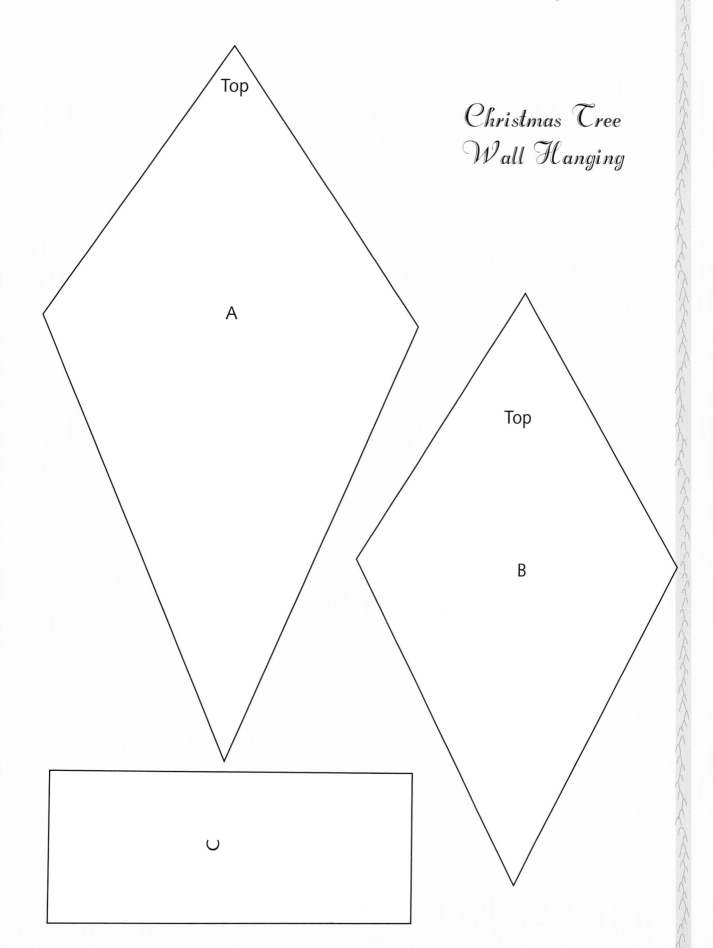

Christmas Tree
Wall Hanging

Top

A

Top

B

C

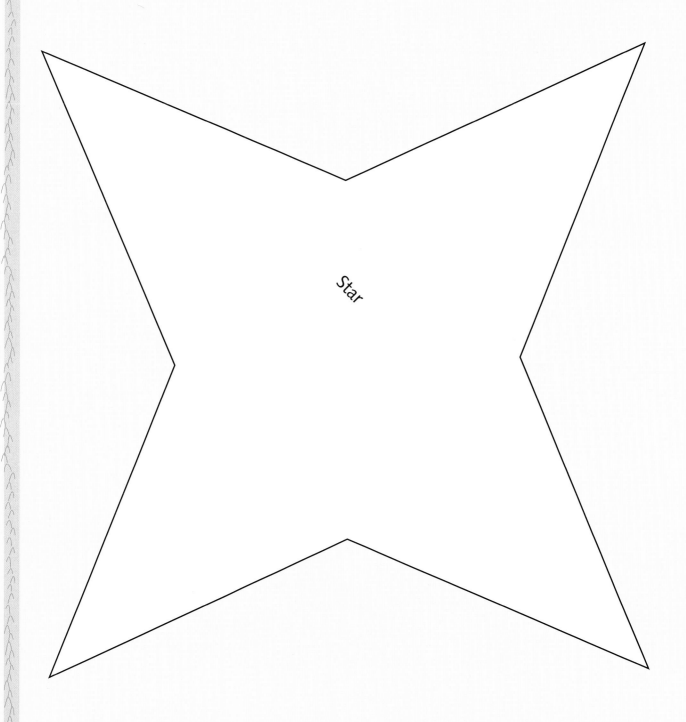

Star

Star Table Runner

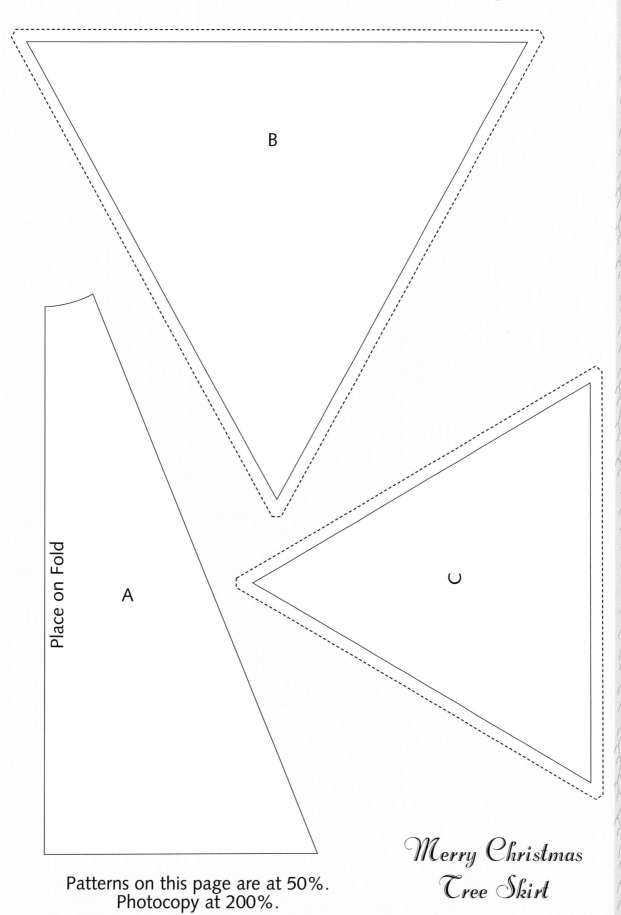

B

Place on Fold

A

C

Patterns on this page are at 50%.
Photocopy at 200%.

Merry Christmas
Tree Skirt

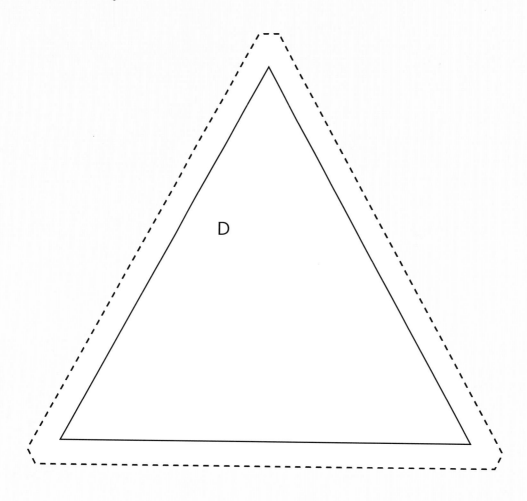

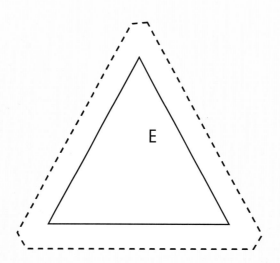

*Merry Christmas
Tree Skirt*

esources

Fabric
Free Spirit
1350 Broadway
21st Floor
New York, NY 10018

Marcus Brothers Textiles Incorporated
980 Avenue of the Americas
New York, NY 10018

Northcott Silk, Inc.
640 Rowntree Dairy Rd.
Woodbridge, Ontario L4L 5T8

Embroidery Floss
The DMC Corporation
S. Hackensack Ave.
Port Kearny Bldg #10F
South Kearny, NJ 07032

Beaded Fringe (Trimtations Beaded Fringe)
Expo International, Inc.
5631 Braxton Dr.
Houston, TX 77036

Buttons (Favorite Findings Button pack)
Blumenthal Lansing Co.
1 Palmer Ter.
Carlstadt, NJ 07072

Picnic Basket
Provo Craft & Novelty
151 E 3450 North
Spanish Fork, UT 84660

Batting and Fusible Web
(Warm and Natural™ Needled Cotton Batting,
Soft & Bright™ Needled Polyester Batting and
Steam-a-Seam 2® fusible web)
The Warm Company
954 E Union St.
Seattle, WA 98122

Rochaille Beads
Hirschberg Schutz
650 Liberty Ave.
Union, NJ 07083

Please support your local quilt, fabric, and craft stores to shop for your supplies. They can give you invaluable service and assistance. Please look and ask for these products.

Meet the Author

Phyllis loves all forms of needlework. She began stitching at a very early age and was taught needlework, sewing, and crochet by her mother and aunt. She would use fabric scraps to design doll clothes. In high school, she sewed some of her clothes.

Phyllis gained a great love and appreciation for quilting from her grandmother's and great-grandmothers' quilts, of which she has several. All of her ancestors quilted and socialized with quilting bees. In addition to her inherited collection of quilts, she searched out other quilts in antique stores and flea markets.

Inspired by her love of needlework, Phyllis began designing professionally in 1984. She formed her own design company, Lucky Duck Designs, and self-published counted cross-stitch leaflets and books for several years. She then switched to freelance designing for books, magazines, and manufacturers so that she could expand and work with many different needlework media. At that time, she taught herself to quilt. She transferred this ability into designing quilts, and has since had numerous quilts published in magazines and books.

Phyllis joined the Embroiderer's Guild of America, and took many technique classes to expand her embroidery skills. She feels that embroidery is important as it can be combined with so many media, especially quilting. She has taught technique classes, and taught and demonstrated at trade shows. Other organizations that Phyllis is proud to be a member of are the Surface Design Association, the Author's Guild, the Society of Children's Book Writers and Illustrators, and the Society of Craft Designers.

Phyllis received a BS degree in Interior Design from the University of Alabama, and lives in Birmingham, Alabama. Her design studio occupies the second floor of her home, and is a constant source of inspiration as it contains a collage of fabrics, fibers, beads, buttons, and wonderful assortments of other materials.

Phyllis invites you to visit and contact her through her Web site, **www.phyllisdobbs.com**.